DEDICATION

To my friends and family, but especially to my loves—Margot, Juliette and John—my arms open wide to you all!

ACKNOWLEDGMENTS

To my mom, for your inspiration, artistic genius and your gift of caring for others.

To Kathy, for always being there, listening to my many ideas and for your quiet strength.

To Heidi and Paul, for the many blessings you have provided me, for giving me a chance, listening to me and for always believing in me.

To Bill and Meg, for your love, warmth, support of all of my endeavors and for believing in me.

To David, for your kindness and your sense of humor.

To Pat and Ellis, for your constant love and support, for the blessings you have given John and me and the children; thank you from the bottom of my heart.

To Tonia, for believing in me, for giving wings to my ideas, but most of all, for your kindness and friendship—for being you—and making my dreams come true!

To Christine, for her incredible talents behind the camera, her kindness and sharing—her laughter. . . .

To Julie, for keeping me on track and organized.

To John, my best friend, confidant, supporter and teacher and of course, my love—you make my heart sing.

To Margot and Juliette, my two little angels, the inspiration behind all of the healing recipes and teas in this book, the sweetest angels a mom could ever hope and wish for.

Thank you all!

CONTENTS

5

PRESCRIPTIONS FROM THE PAST

I was doing a research paper

on *curanderas*—healing women in West Texas—and I had stumbled on a curandera named Milagros who lived there in the 1930s. Milagros, it is said, practiced Miracle Thinking and made jewelry to heal the sick and mentally ailing. I was quite interested in her because I had never before heard of a curandera that used jewelry making in her healing practice. I researched libraries, universities, and the National Parks only to find a few tidbits of information about her. Luckily for me, the ad I put in the local newspaper—*the Big Bend Gazette*—panned out with a lead as to where she had once lived. I called the lead and learned of a cabin up on Wild Horse Mountain, and I took a winding path (barely visible anymore due to all of the overgrowth). Up the path I went until I came to an old adobe house that was quite dilapidated, but I could tell it had been loved long ago. I decided to go in and take a look through the cobwebs and dust. It was here that I spotted the old pre-scription book. Leather-bound, with the names of her patients, illnesses and the how-to infor-mation to make her healing jewelry, it was a gold mine of information, healing-tea recipes, lotions, potions and, most of all, the recipes for the healing treasures themselves. It was while reading this old prescription book that I came up with the idea to share her recipes with you. I have a sense that that is exactly what she would want me to do.

PREPARING FOR HEALING

YOUR OWN CURANDERA PRESCRIPTION BOOK

Just as Milagros used a special book to record her observations, recipes and ideas surrounding the healing power of jewelry, so will you want to have your own Prescription Book. This is where you will record your thoughts and notes about the person you want to help, even if that person is yourself. Other things that can go in your book: herbs you know work well for these types of conditions; the gemstones and colors that correspond to the illness or malady; any objects the person mentions that you may feel could be power objects and any type of thing that rouses emotions within the person. You will jot down thoughts that come to mind while talking with them. It is here that you will design the piece, where you will write down how to make it and what thoughts you were having while you made it. As you may start to see, the prescription book is indispensible.

You can purchase ready-made journals, but I suggest that you make one instead from a composition book. It is a great practice to make your own book because then it is personalized and yours alone. It becomes a special part of your creative heart by making it.

Write the date and year inside of the front cover (or on the spine in metallic marker). Begin the book with your first thoughts on healing or jump right in with your first person you wish to help.

YOU WILL NEED

- standard composition book
- collage elements (leather, fabric, tissue, newspaper, glitter or any embellishment you like from feathers to rhinestones)
- scissors
- acrylic matte medium
- pens, markers, inks, stamps, printing blocks— any mark-making tools that you enjoy using

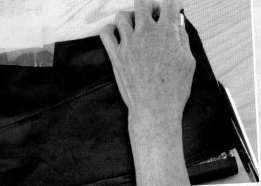

1. Cut out fabric, paper or leather to match the shape of both the front and back cover.

2. Apply matte medium to the cover and adhere your fabric, paper or leather.

3. Layer your embellishments on top of the background. Go as simple or as decorative as you like; it is your prescription book.

Elements to Encourage Healing

The following information on the power of colors and of gemstones/metals would be very helpful to record in your Prescription Book (see page 8) where you can refer to them easily.

Red: An energetic color, a hot color, a protection color and a color to get the blood moving. It lifts your spirit, sense of love, magnetism and good luck. This color is not recommended for angry people, as it can impassion them in the wrong direction.

Blue: A sedate color, cooling, calming. It is a water color and represents truth, harmony and serenity. Blue is good for nervous conditions.

Green: This is a healing color. It is good for growth, calming, and activating energy. Love, hope, generosity, compassion and good health are all associated with green. With the spirit in the right place, it attracts prosperity; however, it is not good for jealous people, or people struggling with greed.

Purple: Royalty, piousness and religion have all long been associated with this color. It offers wisdom and an ability to gain insight. Leadership, enlightenment, understanding, high energy, progress and motivation can all be encouraged with purple. It also gives an ability to overcome bad habits, while increasing self-control. It is not recommended for people with depression.

Yellow: This is an energetic, happy color and can brighten up your constitution. Yellow helps you to speak your mind, and it is a power color. It is a color associated with self-awareness, knowledge, success, creativity, quick luck, activity and intelligence. It is the color of feminine strength.

Orange: This is a creative color and a happy color. It helps remove blocks. It is associated with vitality, success, friendship, attraction and adaptability.

Black: This is associated with the void and represents mystery. In some cultures it is associated with death. It is a color that fades and recedes. It absorbs negative influences, and repels them. Black protects the wearer.

White: This the color of all colors. It is associated with the light. It is associated with purity, goodness and creation. It is a color of strength of the spirit.

Agate: Closely associated with the third eye, the agate symbolizes man's inherent "love of good." Generally considered a lucky stone.

Bone: Said to cure backache, cramps and toothaches.

Brass: Diminishes suffering, represents both the sun and immortality.

Bronze: Encourages strength of character, longevity and relaxation.

Carnelian: Said to help your body absorb vitamins, minerals and nutrients. It also has been known to offer protection from spiders, scorpions and the evil eye, as well as stomach and liver ailments.

Citrine: This helps one define what they want from life. It is thought to be good for circulation and for alleviating depression.

Coral: Said to enhance fertility as well as offer protection from evil. It signifies creative forces, wisdom and deep devotion.

Crystal: This gem is said to increase clarity of thought, wisdom, healing and communication. Also known to hold the secrets of the future.

Garnet: A very powerful gem, this bestows friendship, generosity and potentially long life. It is said to clear the skin, and it also promotes creativity. When worn, the garnet imbues true love and faithfulness.

Pearl: This represents innocence, pureness of heart and fertility, as well as great inner strength. It has been said to ease chest and heart complaints, to cool tempers and to bring understanding.

Silver: A feminine metal, silver enhances the innate power of the one who wears it. It can never be altered by magic. It is associated with the moon, strengthens psychic abilities and cleanses the body of contamination.

Turquoise: A stone very close to the sky, turquoise aids meditation, imparts wisdom, serenity, honesty, friendship, good luck and good health. It is said to offer protection from injury, improve eyesight and bring long life.

Preparing Yourself to Help Others

It can be challenging focusing on the needs of others and determining what it is they truly need, when you are tired, stressed or unable to focus. I think you'll find it helpful to look over this checklist and keep these practices in mind each time you prepare to see a person in need of healing.

GROUNDING

When working with people who are struggling or have assorted ailments, it is a good idea to ground yourself. That is, to protect yourself from any negative or harmful energy patterns, which could otherwise exhaust you and render you less than capable of serving those same people you wish to assist. To do this, you need to focus your energy. Imagine sending a cord into the ground to keep your energies stable. As you send this envisioned cord down into the earth, imagine a force field of light surrounding you. Doing this makes you a much more effective healer. Healers are often empathetic, and they pick up others' energy quite easily. So it is advisable to ground yourself before working with anyone.

QUESTIONS AND LISTENING

Ask the person a lot of questions. What are their needs, what ailment is bothering them, what is their emotional status? What, if any, gemstones are they attracted to? Listen to what they say with all of your senses and jot down anything and everything that comes to mind. Draw designs that come to mind; add colors that you see with your mind's eye; let all of your senses work with you on the design and the design will be sure to heal.

INTENTIONS

When making the piece it is always good to state the intention of why you are making that piece and for what purpose. In this way you are empowering the piece—giving it a sense of purpose. It is advisable to do this with everything you make, as it helps the design become cohesive and much more powerful.

CENTERING

Similar to grounding, centering will quiet the chatter in your mind, relax you and prepare you to focus on either your patient or on the creation process. To center I suggest you face the East and take a deep breath through your nose. Tense your whole body, then, relax with a forceful exhale. Repeat this three times, releasing your body's tension.

Now slowly breathe in through your nose making a snakelike sound in the back of your throat, then, exhale slowly, making the same hissing sound in the back of your throat, while breathing through your nose. This is called uji breath. It slows restless thoughts, releases tension and is great to use when you are feeling stress.

Discovering Treasures

The basement, the attic and Granny's trunk are all great places to find special treasures you might need to incorporate into your healing jewels and remembrance pieces. Other items such as old auto parts, rusty nails, patina tins, rusty tin cans . . . these also make fabulous enclosures for shrines, reliquaries and nichos. When you come across old trade beads, snatch them up; they get harder and harder to come by. When you find glass beads, I suggest roughing them up with sandpaper. It gives them texture and age. Brown shoe polish rubbed into beads ages them, as does burnt umber paint. I often like to age my bone beads in strong coffee grounds for two days. They take on a wonderful tea-dyed appearance.

While hiking I often come across smooth rocks that make for very special power objects. A power object is any object that you feel a connection with. For the smooth rocks, I make wire cages, or I bead a strand of leather and attach it to the rock, or encase it in suede and tie it off. Any of these ideas will work to make your power object a pendant. Think about other ways you might encase objects you find that resonate with you.

Many times the people you wish to help will want vintage pieces incorporated within their healing pieces. Vintage is any piece that dates back fifty years or more. Vintage pieces are getting harder and harder to come by, and many vendors are selling new pieces aged to look vintage. (I have unknowingly fallen for this trick myself more than once.) So my best advice is to start with your client. If they possess a vintage piece of their own, those would be more powerful to them anyway. Ask them to search their things for that object that will form the healing agent in their piece.

When working with new pieces, it is often necessary to age the piece in order for the piece to flow visually. It keeps the eye roaming, and the mind fixed on the intention of the piece. I age most of my pieces as I like the look and feel of the metal when it is aged; it takes on a softer appearance to me, and seems to blend with everything better.

As for aging metal, liver of sulfur is always my first choice. It allows nonferrous metals (copper, silver and brass) to oxidize quickly and take on wonderful hues from brown, to blue, to black. Brass can be placed in a plastic container with cider vinegar and left for a bit to create a wonderful and natural brown patina. Rubbing your pieces in dirt often gives a nice aged feel, too.

Remember collecting your materials takes dedication and perseverance. You will learn which objects tend to bring the prescription needed—which ones bring comfort, and which items will offer its recipient the feeling of protection. Build your medicine bag slowly by watching, listening and questioning.

TOOLS OF THE TRADE

These basic tools should be considered for every curandera's Possibility Bag (see pages 14 and 15). Although you will not need every tool for every project, you never know when it will come in handy in your day-to-day practice of creative healing.

The range of metal we'll be using to create the jewelry in this book includes sterling silver, copper and brass. 24-gauge wire will be the most common wire size, but occasionally we'll use 18-, 20- and 22-gauge as well. For sheet metal, I find 22-gauge to be most workable overall. Most, if not all, of these items can be found at jewelry supply, craft supply, art supply and hardware stores.

Hammers: I love an all-purpose ball-peen hammer, a sledge hammer and a rubber mallet—all found in most hardware stores.

Tin snips: My favorite is the pair that you can buy at a jeweler's supply store that look like ordinary scissors but with smaller blades. They can cut up to 26-gauge metal, but I even cut up to 20-gauge with them.

Wire cutters: These make snipping different gauges of wire as easy as pie. Found at your trusty hardware store, you can also buy ordinary tin snips from the hardware store and they will work absolutely fine for cutting wire.

Jewelry pliers: Round-nose for wire wrapping, making jump rings and ear wires; needle-nose for cinching wire tightly. Both are found at jewelry supply stores or at your local craft store.

Steel block, railroad tie or anvil: You need something hard like this to stamp metal, to flatten it and to give it overall texture, when combined with a hammer and sometimes other tools such as metal stamps.

Wood block: This is used for repoussé work, tin stamping, for support and for drilling holes.

Two stones with a lot of texture: These are great for texturing metal that is "hammered" between the two stones.

Center punch and needle punch: These are used to prepare a hole for drilling and also to stamp metal designs. They are found at hardware stores.

Rotary tool: This is a great all-purpose tool, found at hardware stores. I use a Dremel. You can use it to drill, sand, file, polish, cut and even engrave.

Two-hole metal punch: This tool creates holes in sheet metal in two sizes: $1/16$" (1.6mm) and $3/32$" (2.3mm). It is quick and easy to use when the holes you want to make aren't too far in from the edge of the metal. They are available at jewelry supply stores and over the Internet.

Metal files: Available in numerous grades and sizes, I use mainly a flat file or a finer-tooth file to soften the edges of my metal pieces. When filing, push away from you.

Sandpaper: I follow up my filing with sandpaper, which is available in several grits. A fine-grit (wet/dry 200–400) works well after filing to remove some of the darkening that comes from a patina and brings back a bit of the metal's sheen, unless you are trying to create additional texure on the surface of the metal.

Scissors: For your paper, collaging and fabric projects, a sharp pair of scissors is a must.

Sealer: When using collage pieces in jewelry, be sure to seal your work with polyurethane spray sealer, or something similar. Diamond Glaze gives a great resin-like look to a piece, but matte sealer works well too.

Natural bristle brush: Use one of these to apply patinas and liver of sulfur.

Adhesives: I use epoxies, jeweler's glues and good old craft glue.

Liver of sulfur: Used to blacken or age metal, you can find this in garden stores or through jewelry supply stores. You'll also want a small glass bowl to use the patina in, as well as some latex or similar gloves to protect your hands.

Dust mask: It's good to wear one of these when drilling, sanding or polishing. While the particles may barely seem noticeable to you, over time they can do damage.

Plastic safety glasses: When you are drilling, cutting and punching, these will keep debris from your eyes.

Metal stamps: Found at hardware stores, jewelry supply stores and online, these are available as alphabets or as icon designs.

Tin punches: These can be anything from the lowly nail in different sizes to those that create holes of a specific size. Available online or at some hardware stores.

Embossing tools: These run the gamut from a simple stylus to create lines on metal, to wheels that repeat a pattern. These are easy to find at craft stores.

Epoxy resin: Mixed as a liquid, this can be poured into a bezel where it will harden with a glasslike finish, protecting and encasing whatever you pour it over. Found at hardware stores or craft stores.

Acrylic paints: Collect a variety of colors that you like. You can use these to antique pieces and to paint on cabochons.

Rubber stamps and permanent ink: These are used to etch projects that will go in an etchant solution. StazOn is a good ink to use and is available at craft stores. A permanent marker, such as a Sharpie, will work as well.

Rags and paper towels: For cleanup!

→ MAKE YOUR WORKSPACE BEAUTIFUL

Inspiration will come to you a lot easier if you are happy in the space you choose to create in. Surround yourself with things that make you smile. Use tin cans stamped or punched with designs, old cigar boxes and wine crates for storage. Old glass hors d'oeuvres plates are a great landing place for beads. Display dried flowers or fresh flowers—let your imagination run wild.

Consider using velvet or chamois under your work so that the beads don't roll off the table and you can see what you are aiming for with the piece. Practice stamping and wire wrapping on old metal scraps, brass, or any other inexpensive metal until you get the hang of it. You sure don't want to ruin a piece of sterling or gold. And remember, it is the act of practicing and working that develops your style. I hope you can use these prescriptions as a jumping-off point, and I would sure love to see what healing jewelry you come up with. Please email me a photo of your creation and tell me what you used it for: mariekfrench@gmail.com. Good luck my friend!

POSSIBILITY BAG

Everyone needs a Possibility Bag—a bag where you can dig your hand in and pull out a new adventure, a new way of thinking about something. I won't call it magic . . . but I might hint at magic. Your Possibility Bag is where you will store some of your most frequently used tools and materials. I call it my "house-call possibility bag," as it goes everywhere with me. I have three Possibility Bags, actually. One holds my rubber stamps, punches, repoussé stamps and embossing stamps; one holds my hammers; and one holds my basic tool kit of pliers, tin snips, a few assorted wires and the like. What will your Possibility Bag hold? There is no one right way to make the bag. These instructions are just a jumping-off point. Let your wings fly as you construct your bag of possibilities.

YOU WILL NEED

- two pieces of deerskin or one large piece of leather, or, if you do not want to use animal, faux suede
- leather scissors
- pen to mark holes for punching
- hole punch
- sinew thread or leather cord
- large leather needle (if using sinew)
- beads, charms, talismans or amulets (optional)

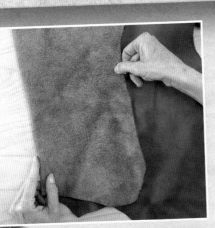

1 Start by folding the leather in half. Fold, unfold and refold until you have the bag shape you would like. Don't worry about odd ends or pieces of leather off to the side. Just find the shape you would like.

2 Cut off any excess leather that you don't want.

3 Mark and hole punch the leather where the pieces will be stitched together.

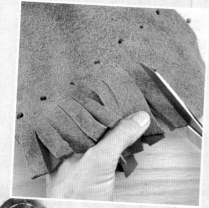

4 Along the bottom, you may wish to place the holes 2" (5cm) up from the edge, to allow you to cut the leather into strips as fringe.

5 Cut several 4" (10cm) strips from the leather cord. Push each piece of leather through two corresponding holes, and tie a knot on one side with the cord.

6 Tie a knot on the reverse side with the remainder of the cord.

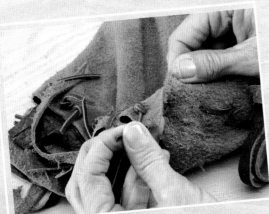

7 Sew the side seams with sinew or leather cord, using a running stitch and knotting the leather at the beginning and end.

8 Cut three 42" (107cm) pieces of leather cord. Braid the leather cord, and attach it to the sides of the bag through a hole you cut on the sides. Knot each braid. Optional: Attach beads, charms, talismans or amulets to the fringe on the bag, decorate it with your personal symbols and remember the possibilities.

BASIC JEWELRY TECHNIQUES

The methods and how-tos are presented here as a way for you to speak life into your materials. You will learn how to wire wrap, stamp onto metal, patina and age a piece—how to make a piece your own.

As you use each step in building your piece, imagine your intention growing from a seed into a fully fledged creation of that intention. Each step will be added onto the next like you are watering the piece with your love. Let the assembly using these simple instructions enhance the process, journey and intention of your creation.

SANDING, FILING AND POLISHING

Many of the pieces will need to be filed, sanded and polished in order to smooth them out, age them and make them soft to the touch.

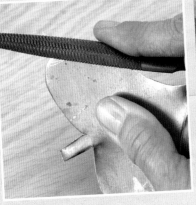

FILING

Select a file appropriate in size to the piece you are to file. Many files will work for many of the pieces. This is a good step for trusting your intuition. File with an action that is away from you as if you are pushing the file. You will develop a rhythm, as if making your own music.

SANDING

Choose wet/dry sandpaper 320–600 grit. 320 sandpaper will remove larger spurs, and then you can progress to higher numbers (indicating a finer grade) as you wish to give your piece a smooth finish. Rub the piece vigorously with the sandpaper.

POLISHING

Get yourself a polishing cloth or chamois cloth. Sunshine makes one with red rouge polish on one side, and chamois on the other. But a simple chamois will work fine. If using the Sunshine cloth, start with the red-rouge side of the cloth and rub vigorously on all sides of the piece. Turn the cloth over and buff the piece to a shiny finish.

CREATING A PATINA

A natural patina is a finish that appears on a piece as it ages. It appears dull and worn, and if it has been used often, loved. I love this finish—tattered, torn and worn. You don't have to wait years for a patina to naturally form on a piece. You can patina a piece using liver of sulfur, sticking it in a container with a boiled egg for quite a few days (does the trick in a stinky way), you can scratch it, sand it, rub it in beeswax polish and rub dirt into it. Use your imagination and let me know what you come up with.

 1 Fill a cup with warm water and place your piece in it.

 2 Pour 1 cup of warmed liver of sulfur liquid into another cup. Move the piece from the water over to the liver of sulfur and dip it in. If when you remove it, it's as black as you'd like, you're done.

 3 If not, leave it in the solution for a few minutes.

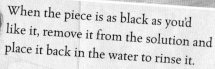 4 When the piece is as black as you'd like it, remove it from the solution and place it back in the water to rinse it.

5 Dry the piece when you're finished.

17

BASIC ROSARY WRAP

I love rosaries, and it is from them that I learned this very basic rosary-wrap technique.

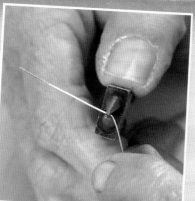

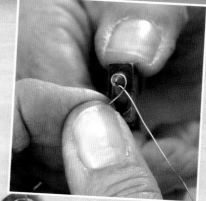

 1 With a length of wire, form a loop using the round-nose pliers at one end.

 2 Bring the wire tail around one of the wire jaws.

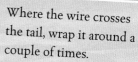 **3** Where the wire crosses the tail, wrap it around a couple of times.

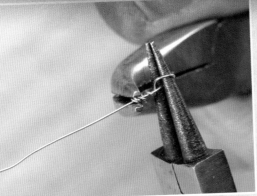

 4 Trim the excess wire tail.

 5 Add a bead.

 Create a loop at the other end.

 Wrap the wire around the shaft until you use all the wire.

MAKING A WIRE-WRAPPED CONNECTION

Connecting two rosary wraps or one wrap to a jump ring is easy. The process is the same as it was for the rosary wrap, only you thread the wire through the loop or ring you're attaching it to before you close the loop.

1 Thread the wire through the joining loop or ring.

2 Wrap the wire around the base of the loop, and trim the excess wire.

MAKING A HOOK CLASP

Making your own hook clasps adds your personal touch to the piece. Many gauges work fine, and the length of wire to start with varies depending upon how large you want your clasp. I usually cut a 2" (5cm), 18-gauge piece of wire to start with.

 1 File the end of the wire by pushing the file away from you in even strokes. This is to remove the pointed bevel created when you cut the wire.

2 Measure a piece between 1½"–4" (4cm–10cm) long (depending on your preference).

3 File the other end of the wire. At one end of the wire, make a loop using round-nose pliers.

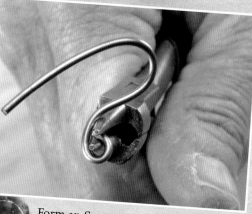

 4 Form an S, wrapping the wire around your finger in the opposite direction of the first loop.

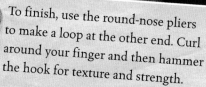 **5** To finish, use the round-nose pliers to make a loop at the other end. Curl around your finger and then hammer the hook for texture and strength.

HAMMERING

Hammers have been used since time immemorial, but I am sure the first time someone needed texture they used a rock. Even though I live in the modern era, I do this because rocks impart a wonderful texture on metal. But back to hammering.

There are many marks that can be made with the simple hammer. Use it sideways, straight on, hard or soft. Use your imagination. See how many marks you can make with the simple hammer (and rock).

FOR TEXTURE

Hammer the metal using a side stroke, front on or use the back of the hammer. If you wish to create swatches of texture, work on scraps of metal to experiment. Mark the metal on the back with a Sharpie and say which hammer you used to make the marks so that you can use the scrap metal as a reminder of the many marks and textures that a simple hammer can make.

FOR STRENGTH

Hammering round wire flat does what's known as work hardening. Use the flat end of a hammer and flatten rings, hooks or clasps.

EMBOSSING WITH A WOOD BLOCK

Embossing dies and plates can be expensive, so I have found a way to save a bit of money by making my own plates.

 1 Line up a male die or decorative metal stamp to a block of wood. Strike the metal with one good blow from a hammer.

 2 Place the metal sheet to be embossed over the indentation that you just made. Use the hammer with a tapping motion to work the die/stamp into the impression.

3 Remove the metal to reveal the embossing.

EMBOSSING WITH DIES

The trick to embossing with dies is to mark the top and bottom of the plate with a permanent marker, and the sides of the male die as well, so that you can place them correctly when the metal is placed on the plate. And remember to never lift the piece when hammering.

 1 Note how the two halves of the die will go together. You may find if helpful to stack the pieces together and draw a line on the two halves with a permanent marker to remind you how they go back together.

 2 Place your metal on top of one half of the die. If you need to, secure the die in a bench vise. Line up your dies, then hammer the die pieces together with a solid blow. Tap until you feel the dies coming together as much as they're going to, never lifting the die until you're finished.

 3 Remove the metal to reveal the embossing.

STAMPING WITH DIES

The trick to stamping with dies and stamps is to mark the top and sides of the stamps and dies with a permanent marker so you can see which way the design is facing before you strike the metal. Keep your hammering solid and hammer in one stroke with a stamp as the image will blur with more than one stroke.

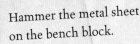 **1** Hammer the metal sheet on the bench block.

 2 View of finished stamp.

3 There are many options for adding stamping with dies. You can play around and see which ones you like best. You can buy punches from the hardware store or from jewelry stores.

22

CREATING JUMP RINGS

Creating your own jump rings is easy and can save you money over pre-made ones. Another bonus is that you can make them match the wire in your project.

1 Begin by coiling wire around a pen, dowel or mandrel that is the size of the rings you wish to create.

2 Using either tin snips or wire cutters, cut through the coil to create individual rings.

3 File the ends of the wire where it was cut, and the rings are good to go! See below for some tips on using them.

OPENING AND CLOSING JUMP RINGS

Jump rings are a necessity in your practice. They are great for loading on amulets and talismans, attaching chain components and dangling earrings. Taking care to close jump rings properly will ensure that you'll never lose a favorite charm or amulet.

1 Using a pair of needle-nose pliers and a pair of bent-nose pliers, grasp the jump ring with pliers, positioning the opening between the pliers.

2 To open, twist the jump ring in a scissors fashion, bringing one set of pliers toward you.

3 To close, bring the jump ring back to the starting position, by twisting in the opposite direction.

HEALING PROJECTS

As I sat on the floor with Milagros' prescription book, I was amazed at the many pieces she had made and the healings she accomplished with her creations. Each recipe or prescription included teas, with the actual plants themselves on the page; the reason she chose the gemstones and watercolor depictions of the stones; the findings sketched and the intent each piece was to have in a fine calligraphic hand. It was like an old herbarium book, filled and stuffed with so many natural treasures.

She had many of the herbarium-type prescription books laid neatly on her dusty floor and still more on the shelves near her couch. There were specimen jars, labeled plants, pressed plants, watercolors of birds and all sorts of rocks and gemstones about her room. There were magnifying glasses, an old microscope and field glasses, gathering bags, insect collections and old implements for healing. It was a magnificent place to be.

I have tried to share within these few pages some of the vast array of recipes Milagros—as a healing woman; a curandera in her day—would, I think, want to share with you my dear friends. I have included some of her techniques, gemstones, findings and teas for healing the body, mind and soul.

As you go forward and make the projects in this book, I hope that you will keep your own intentions and needs in the forefront of your mind when making your projects so that the power of your thought is combined within the healing of each piece you make. May each prescription open up new awareness, and open new ways for you to pass on your own miracles.

NEW BEGINNINGS EARRINGS

January 1, 1924

After every ending, there is always a bright new beginning. Wonderful things are always happening when we are open to receive. In death lies birth. So it is with every New Year. This is the theme for these earrings.

❧ Intention ❦

May I remember that with each small death of my old forms, habits and worries, arises new beginnings, new love and new life.

Materials and why I chose them:

Sterling silver—for its innate power

Rhinestones—light and new beginnings

Bone/shell—bone represents death of the old, and is the fertile ground for new beginnings

Bone also alleviates pain

26

WHAT YOU NEED

- 6mm rhinestone spheres, 6
- sterling silver headpins, 6
- round-nose pliers
- sterling silver Y-shape connectors, 2
- chain-nose pliers
- 24-gauge sterling silver wire
- wire cutters
- sterling silver drops, 2
- bone skull beads, 2
- 6mm rhinestone roundelles, 2
- sterling silver ear wires, 2
- liver of sulfur (optional)

1 Thread one headpin through a rhinestone sphere. Using round-nosed pliers, create a loop at the top of the sphere. Thread the pin wire through one hole in the connector. Secure the loop with chain-nose pliers and wrap the remaining pin wire around the base of the loop. Secure any excess wire and crimp with the chain-nose pliers. Repeat for the other side of the connector with a second sphere.

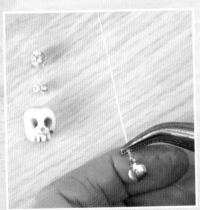

2 Cut a 4" (10cm) length of wire. About ½" (13mm) from one end, create a tiny loop, using round-nose pliers. Thread a sterling silver drop onto the loop, then wrap the remaining tail wire around the base of the loop. Crimp with chain-nose pliers.

3 Thread a skull, then a roundelle, then a sphere onto the wire. Using round-nose pliers, create a loop just above the sphere. Thread the loop onto the center hole of the connector. Wrap the remaining wire around the base of the loop.

4 Trim any excess wire. Using chain-nose pliers, open the ring of one ear wire. Thread it through the top hole of the connector. Use the pliers to then close the loop. Repeat steps 1–4 for the other earring. Patina the earrings in liver of sulfur, if you like. When you wear these earrings, remember that when one door closes another brighter door always opens.

GUIDANCE NECKLACE

January 1, 1924

On this great day of new beginnings, I seek guidance from those who came before me. I know my forefathers and foremothers have battled the same questions, turmoil and circumstances in their own times as I do in mine. Human life is but a drama played out on the celestial stage. So, today, in honor of questions yet unanswered, I make up this guidance necklace. Each one is different as guiding principles for all of us are different. Today I make a necklace featuring Mary, as she signifies to me all that is good, beautiful and true, and I'm sure she can help me find my way.

⇒ Intention ⇐

May the good, the true and the beautiful guide my way.

Materials and why I chose them:
Holy card—as a focus
White feather—thoughts and visions
Pearls—purity and innocence
Rhinestones—light and radiance
Bone—death of the old, fertile new ground, alleviates pain

WHAT YOU NEED

- tin top from lip balm or lid from a baby food jar
- doilies or other decorative paper
- pencil
- scissors
- epoxy glue (E-6000)
- holy card or imagery of your choice
- white feather
- mica
- toothpick
- white glue
- strand of pearls
- beading wire
- wire cutters
- sterling silver crimp beads, 4
- old rhinestone clasp
- crimping pliers
- strand of bone beads: 10mm, about 16" (41cm)
- coffee grounds
- 24-gauge sterling silver wire
- chain-nose pliers
- round-nose pliers

 1 Using a pencil, trace the tin lid onto the doily.

 2 Cut out the circle and glue it into the lid with epoxy. Allow the glue to dry.

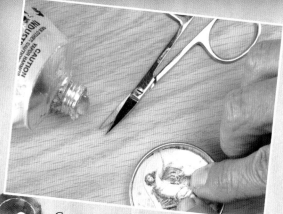

 3 Cut out the figure from the holy card, and glue the figure into the lid on top of the doily. Let the glue dry.

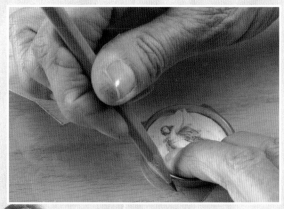

 4 Glue a white feather to the inside of the lid. If you can't find one on a nature walk, it's okay to use one from a down pillow that has been slept on and produced many good dreams.

5 Place a piece of mica on your work surface. Place the lid on top and trace the lid shape with a pencil.

6 Cut out the mica. Using a toothpick, place two small dots of glue on the paper, one on top and one on the bottom.

7 Push the mica into these dots. Let the glue dry, weighing the mica down with marbles, if necessary.

 8 Wrap the strand of pearls around the lid and trim to size.

NAME, NO. & PRICE.   COPY OF PRESCRIPTION.   & PRICE.   COPY OF PRESCRIPTION.

→ NEW BEGINNINGS MEAL

My southern compatriots cook up this delicious meal to ring in the New Year. It is said to bring good luck throughout the year.

Black-Eyed Peas and Collard Greens

Add collard greens, black-eyed peas and ham hock to a pot and boil until the peas pop, signifying good luck and prosperity.

The collard greens signify the color of money, bringing wealth and good fortune. So heap some on a plate and enjoy! May your year be filled with prosperity and good fortune!

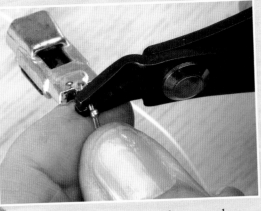

9 Place a bead of epoxy glue around the outside of the lid and attach the trimmed pearl strand. Let the epoxy cure overnight. Cut a length of bead-stringing wire to about 18" (46cm). Thread two crimp beads onto one end, run it through one half of the clasp and then back through the crimp. Use crimping pliers to secure the crimp.

10 Darken the bone beads by leaving them in damp coffee grounds overnight. This will give them a lovely patina. Rinse, and let dry. String the bone beads onto the bead stringing wire until you have about 4" (10cm) of wire remaining.

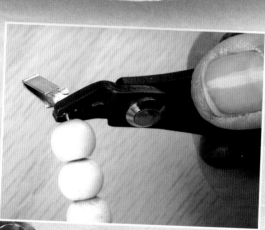

11 Thread the last two crimp beads onto the wire. Run the wire through the other side of the clasp, then thread the wire back through the crimp beads. Crimp the crimp beads, using the crimping pliers, to secure the strand of beads.

12 To attach the pendant, thread a 5" (13cm) length of 24-gauge sterling silver wire between two pearls centered at the top of the pendant. Overlap a 1" (3cm) tail of the wire with the remaining length of wire and as you secure the wires just below the cross section, using chain-nose pliers, wrap the tail around the wires a couple of times. Trim the excess tail wire. Create a loop just above the wrap, using round-nose pliers. Thread the loop over the wire at the center of the bone strand. Holding the loop with chain-nose pliers, wrap the rest of the wire around the base of the loop and crimp the wire to complete, using the chain-nose pliers and a crimp bead. Wear the necklace to bring you guidance when you need it.

CRYSTAL POWER NECKLACE

January 10, 1924

My client Cathy came to me today feeling powerless and victimized. She felt worthless and downtrodden. She was in need of cleansing visions and a new way of seeing herself and her life. This is why I chose crystals. Crystals have always been associated with power, healing and visions. I told her the crystal would give her potent dreams, cleanse her of her old limiting beliefs and help her to see clearly once again. It was with this in mind that I made the crystal power necklace.

⇒ Intention ⇐

I choose to see the situations in my life with clear vision, strength and my innate inner power.

Materials and why I chose them:

Brass—reflects the healing rays of the sun and its strength
Crystal—clarity, healing, power, visions and protection
Rhinestones—light, radiance
Sterling silver—innate power
Vintage rosary—the many hands in prayer
Blue—the color of visions and calming influences

WHAT YOU NEED

- epoxy (E-6000) or jewelry glue
- rough-cut crystal
- brass bullet casing
- awl or engraving tool
- toothpick
- 24-gauge brass wire
- wire cutters
- round-nose pliers
- 24-gauge sterling silver wire
- vintage chain, approximately 24" (61cm)
- rosary chain, approximately 24" (61cm)
- chain-nose pliers
- rhinestone clasp
- dirt

 Glue the crystal into the bullet casing, using jewelry glue or epoxy. Let the piece cure for 24 hours.

 Using an awl or engraving tool, create a design of swirls (or any symbols and motif you like) on the bullet casing.

33

3 Using a toothpick, smear epoxy into the channel at the top of the bullet casing.

4 Cut a length of brass wire to about 8" (20cm) and wrap the wire around the bullet-casing channel four or five times. Bring the two ends of the wire together.

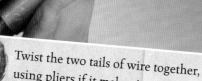

5 Twist the two tails of wire together, using pliers if it makes it easier.

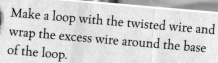
6 Make a loop with the twisted wire and wrap the excess wire around the base of the loop.

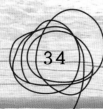

 7 Using 24-gauge silver wire, wire wrap the two vintage chains to the rhinestone clasp using round-nose and chain-nose pliers. (See Making a Wire-Wrapped Connection, page 19.)

8 Using the wire color of your choice, wire wrap the crystal pendant to the center of one of the vintage chains. Bury the necklace in the dirt for three days to cleanse it and prepare it for service. (Ideally, this should be done on the three days of the new moon, as the new moon signifies new beginnings.) Bless this necklace for its healing effects on many ailments, and that it may bring comfort to the wearer.

11080
11080

Vanessa Colnea

PROTECTION AMULET

February 1, 1924

I made these pieces for Mary. They are protection amulets. I wanted Mary to feel secure and to help her release her chronic worries. She has worried for her family and her ability to help provide for them. Trying to find work to earn extra income kept her from spending time with them. Soon Mary was working often enough at odd jobs outside the home that she felt she was losing touch with those she loved and worried about.

It was with this scenario in mind that I made the precious family protection amulets. It's made to bring the family back together, to find common bonds, to see what is truly important in life and to release the dreaded worries—to live once again.

⇒ Intention ⇐

May I remember my family comes first.

Materials and why I chose them:

Lace — we are all fragile
Holy card — all families are holy
Mica — to see things as they really are
Seam binding — to keep the seams of the family bound

WHAT YOU NEED

- lace trim, 24" (61cm)
- aged (tea-stained) seam binding, 24" (61cm)
- hemp string, 24" (61cm)
- epoxy (E-6000)
- ribbon end clasps, 2
- chain-nose pliers
- 28-gauge sterling silver or brass wire
- tin snips or metal shears
- handmade sterling hook closure
- liver of sulfur and a paint-brush
- 20-gauge silver or brass sheet
- round-nose pliers
- imagery from a holy card
- scissors
- mica
- jewelry glue or Diamond Glaze
- 18-gauge copper wire
- hammer
- steel bench block
- ½" (13mm) dowel

1 Stack the lace, seam binding and hemp cord together. Apply a bit of epoxy to the end of the stack.

2 Put one ribbon clasp end clasp over the glued end and crimp closed with chain-nose pliers.

3 Using 28-gauge wire, wire wrap one half of the hook clasp to the end clasp.

4 Repeat steps 1–3 for the other end of the fibers. Tie a single knot with the stack of fibers, and snug it up near the connector.

5 Repeat with a knot on the other end of the strand. Patina some 28-gauge wire in liver of sulfur. Wrap the wire around the fabric at different intervals.

6 Cut a piece of metal sheet to 2" x 1½" (5cm x 4cm). Miter the corners by cutting them off. Find the center of one short side of the box and measure out ¼" (6mm) from either side of the center. At these marks, make a snip in the flashing about ½" (13mm) long.

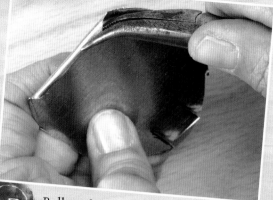

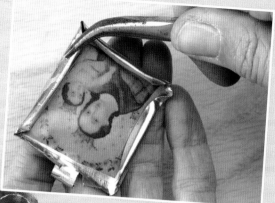

 7 Roll up the bottom of the metal piece using the round-nose pliers.

 8 Cut the imagery on your holy card to about 1½" x 1" (4cm x 3cm). Cut a piece of mica to the same size. Adhere the image to the tin with a tiny bit of epoxy, then, adhere the mica to the top of the image using a couple dots of jewelry glue or Diamond Glaze at the edges. Roll the edges of the sides of the box inward, rolling them just over the edge of the mica/image to help it stay in.

9 Roll in the right and left sides of the top toward the center.

10 Roll the middle piece at the top, toward the back, to form a bail.

39

11 Cut a 4" (10cm) length of 18-gauge wire. Patina the wire using liver of sulfur and a paintbrush.

12 Place the wire through the rolled bail of the pendant.

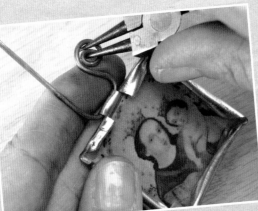

13 Center the wire in the bail, and bend the protruding wires straight up. Spiral both wire ends using round-nose pliers.

14 Flatten the spirals using a hammer on a bench block.

15 Patina the whole piece with liver of sulfur and a paintbrush.

16 Wrap 18-gauge wire around a ½" (13mm) dowel, about four times. Using wire cutters, snip the coil to release two jump rings. (See Creating Jump Rings, page 23.) Hammer the jump rings to flatten them.

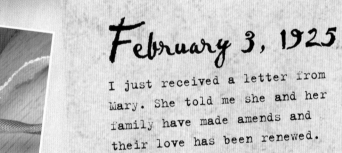

17 Using two pair of pliers, use the jump rings to hang the pendant from the fabric strand, securing them on the spiral bail. Say a blessing to ensure the protection of the wearer.

February 3, 1925

I just received a letter from Mary. She told me she and her family have made amends and their love has been renewed.

41

February 28, 1925

Individuals come to me from time to time asking for special reliquaries for someone who is ill. As each case is different, each reliquary is different. The one I shall make today is for a woman's mother who is ill in the hospital. She needs something small to hold onto to keep her thoughts in alignment with healing. This necklace can bring so much comfort. The prayer beads offer something for the person in need of healing to do with their hands and a way to focus their minds on healing. So with this purpose in mind I got to work.

⇾ Intention ⇽

As I turn each bead, I invoke healing and wellness in mind, body and soul.

Materials and why I chose them:
Sacred heart of healing—symbol of healing and love
Sterling silver—innate love
Power word or phrase—keep me focused on healing
Hand charm—love's helping hand
Silver beads, rosaries—innate power and many prayers

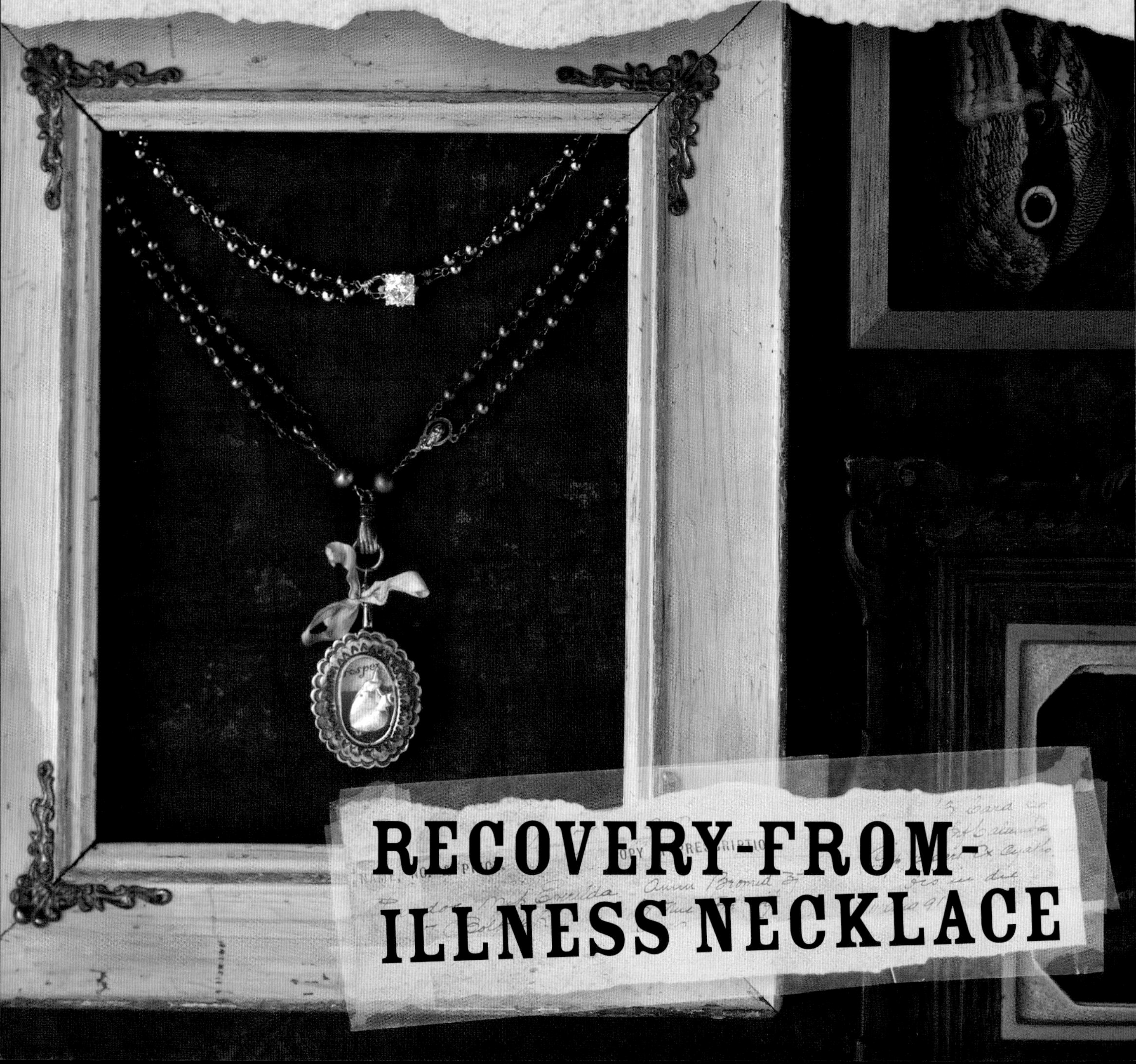

RECOVERY-FROM-ILLNESS NECKLACE

WHAT YOU NEED

- jeweler's glue
- Sacred Heart or other appropriate Milagros
- sterling silver glass-front locket
- toothpick
- paintbrush
- liver of sulfur
- special word, prayer or phrase (I printed out the word **prospero** [prosper] in Black Adder font)
- scissors
- coffee, tea or burnt umber acrylic paint (thinned with water) to age the paper
- chain-nose pliers
- silver rosaries, 2
- round-nose pliers
- 24-gauge silver wire
- silver beads, 2
- hand charm
- small pink ribbon (aged with coffee, if desired)
- rhinestone clasp

→ COMFORTING CREAM

- Mexican vanilla beans
- shea butter
- jojoba oil
- strainer
- glass jars

Place split vanilla beans into the jojoba oil and let steep for thirty days. After thirty days, strain the oil from the beans.

Add one-part vanilla oil to three-parts shea butter and heat to a creamy consistency as you stir it together. Pour into glass jars and let cool to harden.

Try this healing topical cream during times of anxiety. When rubbed between your hands, the scent and soft feel will calm you.

 Add jeweler's glue to the back of the sacred heart Milagros. Drop the Milagros into the locket and use the toothpick to press it into the locket's back wall.

 Using a paintbrush, apply liver of sulfur solution to the metal portion of the locket.

 Cut out your word, phrase or prayer. Age the paper a bit, if you like, by either staining it with tea, or coffee or using a burnt umber paint wash. Glue the aged paper to the top, inside of the locket. Use a toothpick to burnish the paper down.

4 Using chain-nose pliers, remove the drop-pendant portions from the two rosaries.

5 Using the round-nose pliers, wire wrap a silver bead to the pendant connector on each rosary. Wire wrap both silver beads to the hand charm, again, using round-nose pliers.

6 Wire wrap the locket to the hand charm using the round-nose pliers.

7 Tie the vintage ribbon onto the wire-wrapped portion of the locket.

8 Find the center of each rosary, opposite the end of the pendant connection, and wire wrap one half of the rhinestone clasp to each strand, between the beads.

HAVE FAITH NECKLACE

March 26, 1924

Today a woman called me in much distress; I could barely understand her. She had recently delivered a premature baby who was given a small chance at survival. I told her everything would work out if she could keep her being strong. I told her there were two teas I wanted her to drink: Sage Tea and Pau d Arco. The Latinos say that the latter is a miracle tea. I told her to say a blessing for the strength and well-being of her son before every cup.

The final step, I told her, was faith. I said I would send her a necklace to remind her of the force behind that word, for where there is faith there can be no fear.

➤ Intention ←

May I remember to keep my faith strong, knowing that all good comes to those that believe.

Materials and why I chose them:
Sterling silver—innate power
Conchos—circular mandalas
Turquoise—healing and reminder the sky's the limit
Pearls—purity
Religious medals and charms—a feeling of protection, healing and care

WHAT YOU NEED

- tin snips
- 20-gauge silver sheet
- two-hole punch or $^1/_{16}''$ (2mm) punch
- hammer
- metal letter stamps
- circle copper disks, 1" (3cm), with ovals cut out of the centers (see pages 60 and 61), 2
- conchos, ¾" (19mm)
- conchos, ½" (13mm)
- 24-gauge silver wire
- 10mm silver ball beads
- chain, two 3" (8cm) lengths
- small turquoise beads, 2
- small pearl beads, 3
- round-nose pliers
- handmade clasp (see page 20)
- 2" (5cm) chain for medal in the back of the necklace
- religious medals that are appropriate for your faith

1 Using tin snips, cut a rectangle from the silver sheet that is approximately 1½" x 2½" (4cm x 6cm). Punch a hole on each short end of the rectangle, using a two-hole punch or $^1/_{16}''$ (2mm) punch and hammer. Stamp the word faith onto the sheet while setting the intention that the wearer will grow in faith with this necklace.

2 Stamp designs that mean something to you on all of the disks, including the copper disks. As you stamp, affirm your faith in all things good.

46

 3 Using a two-hole punch or ⅟₁₆" (2mm) punch and hammer, create holes on two opposite sides of all the disks and conchos. Wire wrapping assorted pieces (silver ball, chain, conchos, disks, beads) together, using round-nose pliers, create one length of necklace, approximately 9½" (24cm), then add one half of the clasp. Repeat for the other half of the necklace so you end up with two pieces of equal length.

4 Wire wrap one copper disk to each half of the necklace. Near one half of the clasp, also attach a 2" (5cm) chain with a religious medal. (I suggest Michael, the guardian angel.)

5 At the holes on the stamped rectangle, wire wrap two medals, using round-nose pliers, that are meaningful for you and your faith. Finally, wire wrap the rectangle to the two copper disks.

July 1, 1924

The woman with the premature baby wrote me to say that her baby was fine. He was thriving unbelievably. His weight is now that of a boy his age. She also mentioned that the doctors could not believe how well he is doing and how strong he is.

Just goes to show you what a little faith can do.

MY LIFE, MY ALTAR NECKLACE

April 20, 1924

On this Easter Sunday and the beginning of spring, I have made a piece to honor that my life be my altar. It is how we live our lives that speaks volumes to our soul, to others and to the universe. If we lived our lives as if they were our altars, would we not strive to live as the true, loving beings that we truly are?

⇒ Intention ⇐
May my life be my altar.

Materials and why I chose them:
Altar pendant—anything that signifies the good, the beautiful and truth
Mica—fragility of life
Charms—add charms that have personal meaning to you, as the cross (four directions, guidance, strength) and silver disc (cyclical nature) did for me
Sterling silver—innate power
Flower connectors—beauty

WHAT YOU NEED

- two-hole punch or ¹⁄₁₆" (2mm) punch, hammer and steel block
- vintage altar pendant (with doors that open)
- mica
- fine-tip permanent marker
- scissors
- epoxy (E-6000)
- filigree (that fits inside of the pendant channel)
- toothpicks
- small charm, such as a cross or other meaningful icon
- spring clamps
- jewelry glue
- handmade clasp (see page 20)
- 24-gauge sterling silver wire
- round-nose pliers
- 3" (8cm) sterling silver chain with charm
- oval sterling silver disks 18mm x 13mm, 2 (stamped using decorative metal stamps)
- ¾" (19mm) disks, 2 (stamped using decorative metal stamps)
- flower connectors, 2
- 4" (10cm) pieces of sterling silver chain, 2
- needle-nose pliers

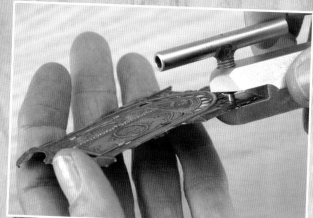

 Using a two-hole punch (or a ¹⁄₁₆" [2mm] punch, hammer and steel block), punch a hole near both top corners of the altar piece.

 Place the altar over a piece of mica, open the doors and, using the marker, trace the opening of the window onto the mica.

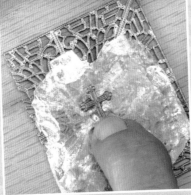

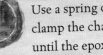

3 Cut the mica shape out with scissors, cutting just slightly outside of the line, so that it won't fall through the window. Using epoxy, glue the mica to the filigree piece.

4 Apply a bit of epoxy to the charm, using a toothpick, and glue the charm to the center of the mica.

5 Use a spring clamp to clamp the charm in place until the epoxy cures.

6 Using a toothpick, apply the jeweler's glue along the channel in back of the altar doors.

7 Set the filigree piece against the glue, and clean up any excess glue with a toothpick.

8 Using two clamps, clamp all the pieces together (with the doors open), and allow the epoxy to cure for 24 hours.

9 To assemble the chain, begin with one half of the clasp. Start a wire wrap using round-nose pliers. Before closing the first loop, string on the piece of clasp. Wrap the tail and create a second loop. Thread on one length of chain and complete the wire wrap. Drill holes on opposite sides of the disks and ovals. To the other end of the chain, wire wrap a flower connector, an oval disk and a round disk.

10 Repeat for the other half, only before closing the second loop, thread on the piece of dangle chain with the charm.

11 Wire wrap the altar piece to the bottom of the chains. Wear this necklace when you need a gentle reminder to make your life your altar. It comes in quite handy on those mornings when you are not quite feeling your true self and are having a hard time appreciating the gift of a new day.

STRENGTH-OF-HEART NECKLACE

WHAT YOU NEED

- 18-gauge sterling silver wire
- wire cutters
- round-nose pliers
- hammer
- steel bench block
- 6mm sterling silver jump rings, 17
- file
- liver of sulfur
- sandpaper
- tin sacred heart
- 20-gauge sterling silver wire
- chain-nose pliers

August 24, 1924

I got a letter today from a good friend—Cecilia. She wrote about her need for rejuvenation. She has been volunteering at a hospital working with those that have only a few months, at best, left to live. She told me how she is starting to feel depleted and worn down, and that she needs her energy to be strong for these people. It seems to me she gives a piece of her heart everyday. I feel I should make her a Strength-of-Heart Necklace to recharge her and keep her heart strong in all she does.

❧ Intention ❧

May my sacred heart remain open and strong. May I remember a life is lived when tiny gifts of love are shared.

Materials and why I chose them:
Sterling silver—innate power
Tin heart—honored for its strength and fragility

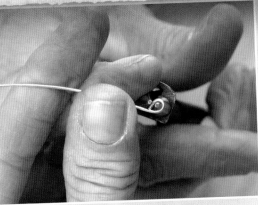

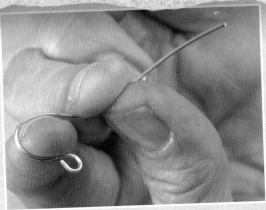

 1 Cut nineteen 3" (8cm) pieces of 18-gauge wire. Begin with one piece of wire. Use round-nose pliers to turn a tiny loop at one end of the wire.

 2 Bend the wire up and around your finger. This creates an elliptical shape, instead of a circular shape.

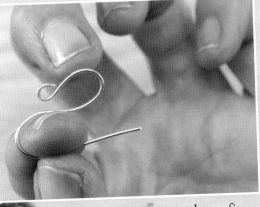

 3 Now, curve the wire around your finger again, but in the opposite direction, to begin forming a figure eight.

4 Using round-nose pliers, create another tiny loop at the remaining end of the wire.

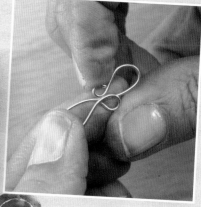

➜ ROSE-COVERED TISSUE PAPER

Pick roses on the full moon when they are at the height of their bloom. Lay out the roses on a screen in a dark closet or attic and allow warm air to dry them. (It takes about a week or so.)

With a handful of dried rose petals and some white tissue paper, begin gluing petals to the tissue, using a drop of glue on the back of each petal. Continue gluing down petals until the paper is covered. Then, spray the petals with a light coat of varnish to seal the rose petals.

 Using your fingers, squeeze the loops so they meet up in the center, and make a tight figure eight.

 Hammer the figure-eight link on a steel block.

Repeat steps 1–6 to make a total of nineteen figure-eight pieces. Make seventeen jump rings from 18-gauge wire. (See Creating Jump Rings on page 23.) To create a hook, start with another 3" (8cm) length of 18-gauge wire. Create a tiny loop on one end, with round-nose pliers, and, once again, curve the wire around your finger. Now flatten the loop a little bit.

Bend the wire up, approximately 90 degrees.

 Trim the excess wire, leaving about ¼" (6mm) of wire after the bend.

NAME

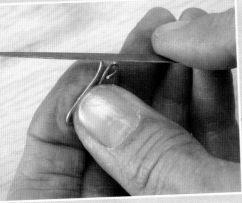

 10 File the cut end of the hook so that it isn't sharp.

 11 Using the hammer and bench block, hammer the hook to work harden it.

 12 Patina all the metal pieces and polish as desired, using sandpaper. To assemble the two halves of the chain, connect the links using the jump rings. (See Opening and Closing Jump Rings on page 23.) Create one length of chain with nine links, and one with ten. To the shorter chain, add the hook using the round-nose pliers.

 13 Wire wrap the heart to the ends of the chain, using 20-gauge wire and round-nose pliers and chain-nose pliers.

After I finished the necklace for Cecilia, I wrapped it in paper that I glued dried rose petals onto. I sent her the package and she sent me a letter back saying that she never felt better. She wrote small notes on the rose tissue paper and gave them to her patients. Most kept the notes under their pillows for strength. She said her heart was renewed and thanked me.

CIRCLE-OF-LIFE EARRINGS AND BRACELET

August 26, 1924

It is a hot and especially blustery day. The winds are blowing hot air, and the sun is oppressive. I am feeling too hot, and I am extremely grouchy. It is time I snap out of it. I have to remind myself that seasons come in circles; life comes in circles and time changes in circles. To remind myself of this I quickly made up these earrings and bracelet.

⇜ Intention ⇝
May I remember that life is cyclical.

Materials and why I chose them:
Sterling silver—innate power
Circle—life is cyclical, circles are protective and all-encompassing

Earrings

1 Cut a 4½" (11cm) piece of sterling silver wire. Hammer the wire flat. At one end, use round-nose pliers to make a loop.

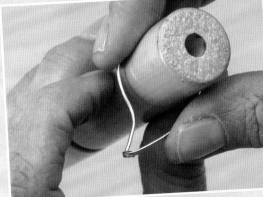

2 Bend the opposite end of the wire about ½" (13mm) from the end. Shape the wire around the dowel to form a circle.

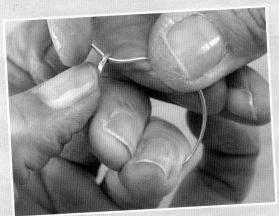

3 Check to see the tension is right so that the bent portion will be able to be threaded through the loop to close the earring.

WHAT YOU NEED

- 18-gauge sterling silver wire
- wire cutters
- hammer
- steel bench block
- round-nose pliers
- 1" (3cm) dowel
- 8mm sterling silver beads with large holes, 5
- liver of sulfur (optional)
- bracelet mandrel or spray can
- pencil or similar size dowel

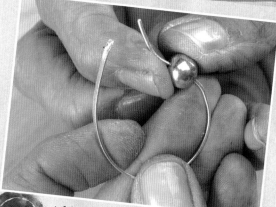

4 Add the sterling silver bead onto the hoop. Repeat steps 1–3 to create a second earring. Patina the earrings in liver of sulfur, if desired.

Note: Before wearing the earrings, set an intention that you will remember that all of life is cyclical.

57

Bracelet

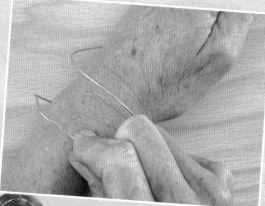

 1 Cut an 18" (46cm) piece of sterling silver wire. Hammer the wire to give it some texture. Wrap the wire several times around a bracelet mandrel or spray can. Try the coil on to make sure it fits.

2 Coil one end of the wire around a pencil, three or four times.

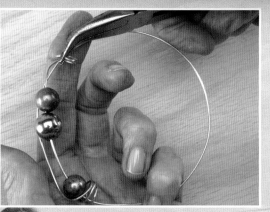

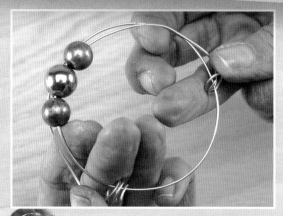

3 Thread on three silver beads, threading each rotation of the wire through the beads. Take the beads and attach them from the other side, circling them to the center.

4 Coil the other end of the wire around the pencil, then spiral the coil around the wire of the bracelet to close it. Patina the bracelet in liver of sulfur, if desired.

BELIEVE-IN-MYSELF BRACELET

August 28, 1924

Frida came over today to spend some time chatting. We often like to sit outside and visit over tea. I have known her for many years, as we met at school way back when. She feels stuck in her art and life today. I told her it is only because she is impatient! She laughed at me. I told her she needed to believe in herself and the process. That, she said, was easy for me to say. I said, "Oh yeah?" We both laughed.

I told her that we would both work on a Believe-in-Myself bracelet. She was agreeable. So this is what we did.

❧ Intention ❧

As the author of my life, what do I want to portray? I intend to portray life at its most full.

Materials and why I chose them:
Copper—a conductor of energy
Sterling silver—innate power
Stamping—a way to use personal symbols:
circle—cyclical nature; what comes around goes around
circle with rays—the inner light in each of us
cross—four directions
flowers—beauty
dots—marks we make daily—good and bad

WHAT YOU NEED

- permanent marker
- 18-gauge copper sheet
- tin snips
- two-hole punch or $^1/_{16}$" (2mm) punch
- jeweler's saw
- file
- sandpaper
- hammer
- steel bench block
- assorted metal stamps
- 1" (25mm) brass disks, 2
- ¾" (19mm) sterling silver disks, 2
- liver of sulfur (optional)
- 20-gauge sterling silver wire
- handmade hook clasp (see page 20)
- round-nose pliers
- chain-nose pliers

 1 Draw an oval onto the copper sheet. Then draw a second oval inside the first one. Cut out the large oval using tin snips or a jeweler's saw.

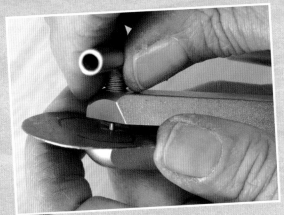

2 Using the two-hole punch, create a hole inside of the inner oval.

→ **MINT AND LICORICE INFUSION TEA**

- a few leaves of spearmint or peppermint
- a pinch of ground licorice
- a pinch of aniseed
- a pinch of fennel
- lemon slices

Pour boiling water over the herbs and let steep for three minutes. If you want a cold infusion, pour cold water over the plants and let steep for a few hours. Filter, add a slice of lemon and enjoy. This tea is great for camaraderie as well as feelings of confidence and strength.

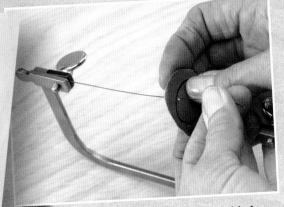

 3 Disengage one end of the saw blade and thread it through the hole in the copper disk. Re-engage the blade into the saw, making certain it is strung tightly.

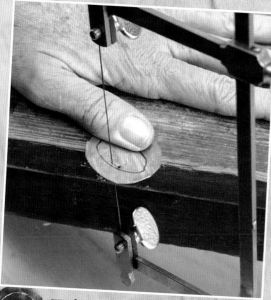

 Working on a bench pin or off the edge of your workbench, use the saw to cut out the inner hole.

 File, sand and polish the round edges. Stamp the metal pieces as desired, using metal stamps and a hammer. Think of symbols that represent who you are or where you want to be.

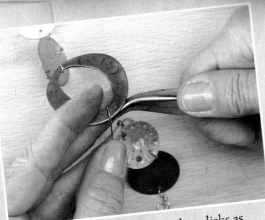

 Stamp the brass and silver disks as well. Patina and polish the metal pieces, as desired. Drill holes on both sides of each disk, using either the two-hole punch or the $\frac{1}{16}$" (2mm) punch and a hammer. Wire wrap the disks together through the punched holes to create the bracelet.

Note: As you assemble the bracelet, keep in mind the following intention: May my life symbols remind me to believe in myself.

Wire wrap the hook and the jump ring onto the ends of the bracelet.

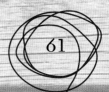

FORGIVENESS NECKLACE

September 14, 1924

I see changing skies. The fish scales are the tell-tale sign. That sky is called a mackerel sky. I had a feeling that my next guest would be looking for a change in her life, and indeed she did.

Some time ago, her best friend took her fian-cée away. She was to be married in a week, and he announced that he did not love her but he loved her friend instead. It has been several years now, but she has not been able to get over it.

I first made her a blend of my Forgiveness Tea, then I told her how we were going to create a necklace together—one that would allow her to release her feelings of betrayal, so she could begin to forgive.

⇒ Intention ⇐
I forgive the past hurts and disappointments just as the moon wanes and waxes.

Materials and why I chose them:
Sterling silver—innate power to forgive; made on the new moon to signify new beginnings

WHAT YOU NEED

- permanent marker
- 20-gauge sterling silver sheet
- tin snips or metal shears
- file
- sandpaper
- chamois cloth
- two-hole punch or ¹/₁₆" (2mm) punch
- hammer
- steel bench block
- assorted sizes of silver disks and conchos (21 or so)
- decorative metal stamps
- 24-gauge sterling silver wire
- round-nose pliers
- chain-nose pliers
- sterling silver chain
- liver of sulfur (optional)

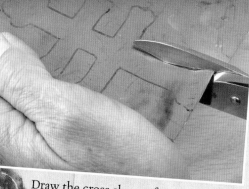

1 Draw the cross shape of your choice onto the sheet metal with a marker. Using tin snips or metal shears, cut out the cross shape.

2 File and sand the edges and polish the cross (see Sanding, Filing and Polishing on page 16). Using the punch, punch a hole at the top of the cross. Using the hammer and bench block, hammer the cross to create texture.

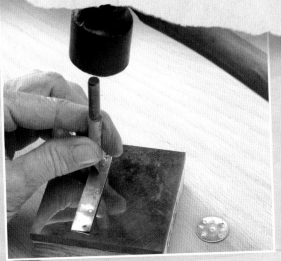

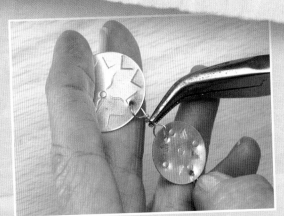

3 Using the hole punch, punch holes on opposite sides of the disks. Embellish the disks and conchos as desired, using the metal stamps. From the metal sheet, cut a strip that is about ½" x 2" (13mm x 5cm) and add texture to it as well.

4 Connect nine of the disks by wire wrapping them together, using the jewelry pliers.

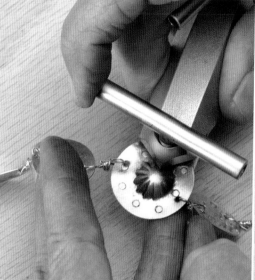

 5 Punch a third hole in the side of the center disk.

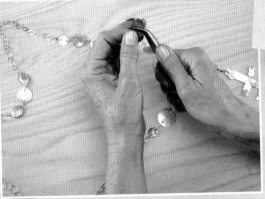

 6 To the new hole, wire wrap three smaller disks and the cross pendant, creating a Y shape.

→ FORGIVENESS TEA

- green tea leaves
- lemon
- lime

Steep tea leaves in hot water for several minutes, then squeeze in fresh lemon and lime juices. This tea is very cleansing and helps us to forgive and forget our past hurts.

7 Add the chain and remaining disks in any fashion you desire. I like to wire wrap a few disks, then some chain, then a few more disks... make the flow your own. Continue adding discs and chain until you reach the opposite side of the Y shape and have a length of about 36"–41" (91cm–104cm).

8 Intersperse the conchos where you see fit. Patina the necklace in liver of sulfur and polish, as desired.

MILAGROS

September 23, 1924

As the new moon and the autumn equinox are on the
exact same day today, I decided that it is apro-
pos to intend miracles to be granted us all. Every
equinox and solstice I enjoy spreading miracle
thinking around the world. Each quarter of the year,
I make up special miracle pieces to pass along to
others so that they, too, can think in miracles. My
name, Milagros, is Spanish for miracles. Milagros
are small pot metal talismans created in an end-
less variety of shapes and sizes, just as miracles
come in all shapes and sizes. When I make and use
Milagros, I become a vehicle for healing, and miracles do indeed happen.

≫ Intention ≪
I pass it on, I pass it forward, its birth is certain.

Materials and why I chose them:
Copper—a conductor of energy
Heart—love

WHAT YOU NEED

- wood or other dimensional heart shape
- 36-gauge copper, brass or tin sheet
- tin snips or metal shears
- metal files
- foam rubber or similar cushy surface
- metal embossing tools
- dapping block
- embossing wheel
- two-hole punch or $^1\!/_{16}$" (2mm) punch, hammer and steel block
- ribbon
- liver of sulfur
- sandpaper

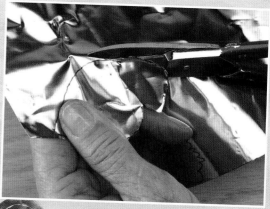

 1 Using your wood or other heart shape as a guide, cut out a loose and slightly larger shape from the copper sheet, using tin snips or shears.

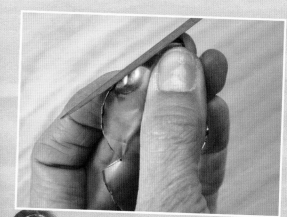

2 File the rough edges.

 3 Place the heart shape down on the foam surface. Put the copper piece on top of it, and using a ball-tipped embossing tool, trace around the shape of the heart.

 4 After you have outlined the basic shape, turn the copper over and set it carefully over a large hemisphere in the dapping block. Use a round-tipped tool to refine the concave shape of the heart.

5 Turn the heart back over and replace it on the foam. Run an embossing wheel around the perimeter of the heart.

6 Using a stylus, create the outline of flames at the top portion of the heart.

7 Using the stylus tool, make dots around the heart. To do this, twist the stylus tool to make the dot.

8 Using another embossing wheel, outline a second heart onto the piece. Using a two-hole punch, make a hole in the top for the ribbon. Use liver of sulfur solution to patina the Milagros and polish it, as desired, using sandpaper. Give the Milagros its mission, its intention.

9 Thread ribbon through the hole and tie so that you can hang it.

MILAGROS BRACELETS

Pass these out often and with the intent of passing on miracles to every recipient.

Materials and why I chose them:
Small Milagros charms—small miracles, healing, protection, wealth, wishes granted

NAME, NO. & PRICE.   COPY OF PRESCRIPTION.

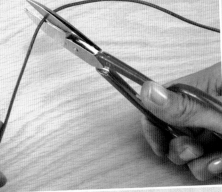

1 Cut a piece of leather cord to a length that, when joined, you can comfortably get over your hand (7"–8" [18cm–20cm]).

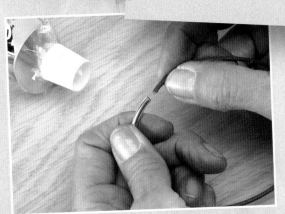

2 Put a drop of epoxy on one end of the leather cord. Slide the cord into the silver tube. Repeat for the other end of the leather.

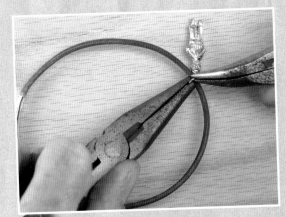

3 Using chain-nose pliers, crimp the ends of the tube shut.

4 Attach the Milagros to the bracelet with a jump ring, using chain-nose pliers. (Using two pairs at once makes the job easier.) If you like, brush liver of sulfur solution on the silver portions of the piece to give it some age.

MILAGROS CARDS

I pass out miracle cards wherever I go. I sneak them into libraries, stores, parks, the post office—anywhere. On these blank postcards, I include a message instructing that they can be collaged, painted, drawn or written on. They serve as prayer cards, petitions and small paper *ex-votos*, or miracle paintings. I usually stamp "postcard" onto the back and I ask that they send them to me so that I can post their miracles on the wall I have for miracles wished for and granted. Pass them out, share, draw and write/create your own miracles.

MILAGROS EARRINGS

Milagros are added to these simple hoops using wire wraps. Attach one or many for those that are in dire need of miracles. You can even personalize these earrings with Milagros that are particular to each person's needs, such as clear vision (eyes), love (a figure or heart), protection (a praying figure) and so on. It all boils down to miracle thinking.

69

CONFIDENCE NECKLACE

September, 30, 1924

Alexandria came by today and told me that she felt creatively blocked. She fears that her work will not be accepted, that she won't have an audience—a chance to share the gifts that she has. She doubts that what she does is any good at all. I told her that many creative people are fearful of this. So I prescribed a special tea recipe, and a necklace for confidence.

I told her that sometimes we need a jolt to get us out of our negative frames of mind. To force us to refocus and see the gifts we have to offer in a new light. Never let doubt cover your eyes, speak into your ears or hold your hands back. Doubt is a strong, dark force, because with doubt comes apathy and inaction. Without action and creation, darkness prevails. But in every act of creation lies a spark of light.

⟩ Intention ⟨

As I wrap each charm, I think thoughts that correspond to the opening of creativity: doors opening, divine guidance, how creations will serve . . .

Materials and why I chose them:
Cross—directional
Rhinestones—light
Bone—removal of pain
Brass—strength of the sun

 1 Patina all pieces in liver of sulfur. Let the bone bead sit in coffee until it's aged looking. Rinse all pieces and allow to dry. Put epoxy into the channel cross, using a toothpick.

 2 Use the toothpick to add rhinestones to the epoxy in the channel cross. Let cure.

 3 Using the rubber mallet, flatten the mesh chain.

4 Measure the flattened mesh around the bone bead, and trim the mesh to fit.

WHAT YOU NEED

- patina solution, such as liver of sulfur
- carved bone bead
- coffee
- epoxy (E-6000)
- channel cross
- toothpick
- 2ss rhinestones
- rubber mallet
- ¼" (6mm) brass mesh chain, about 4" (10cm)
- tin snips or metal shears
- spring clamps
- snake chains in brass or sterling silver, 3
- cord end caps, 6
- chain-nose pliers
- handmade sterling silver S hook (see page 20)
- 24-gauge silver wire
- sterling silver charms that have positive meaning to you
- brass charm to remind you of confidence

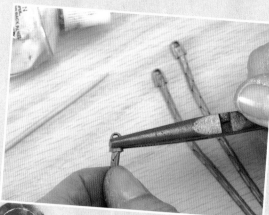

5 Apply epoxy to the four sides of the bead and wrap the mesh over the glue. Using two clamps, clamp the wire mesh to the bead so the mesh is flush on all sides.

6 Glue the three chains into the end caps with epoxy. Using chain-nose pliers, crimp the caps. Let all glued pieces cure fully.

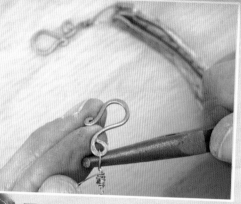

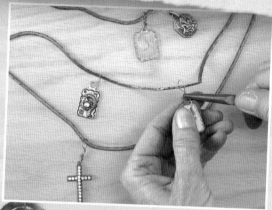

7 Wire wrap the two halves of the S clasp onto the three snake chains.

8 Wire wrap the charms onto the snake chains—one per chain.

→ TEA OF FAITH

- peppercorns crushed under the feet of a strong and confident man
- fresh ginger root slices
- cardamom stars crushed in a stone mortar
- cinnamon sticks crushed in a stone mortar
- pinch of chili pepper
- black tea leaves
- milk
- dash of honey

Steep the first five ingredients in boiling water for five minutes. Strain and add milk and honey. Sip slowly.

October 30, 1924

Alexandria sent me a note and enclosed a small snake charm. She explained that the book she had been laboring over seemed to take on new light when she started it again, and now it is going to be published! She is also scheduled to give lectures in three states within the next three months: Another miracle in faith.

PROSPERITY BRACELET

October 1, 1924

Francesca is having severe financial difficulties and is on the verge of, not only bankruptcy, but also a nervous breakdown. She needs me to help her to recover her balance and remind her of abundance thinking. First I will prescribe for her some Stress-Away Tea.

After she was calm, I explained that she needs to selflessly give something away each month. It is a natural law; that which you give is returned tenfold.

Before creating a bracelet for her, I gave her twelve blank postcards—four for her mind, four for her body, four for her spirit. I told her to create a collage on each one, keeping good thoughts of intention on each as she creates what she wants in the three categories. I told her she is to post them in prominent spots where she will see them every day. She is to meditate on them, picturing herself in each situation until there is a vague transparency between her thoughts and reality. Then she is to mail me the card once it has become a reality.

After that, I began to create her bracelet, as a reminder that she is always wealthy in mind, body and spirit.

73

⇒ Intention ⇐

A prayer to connect each coin to the bracelet, to bring prosperity and calm abundance.

Materials and why I chose them:

Old coins—wealth

Brass—strength of the sun

WHAT YOU NEED

- brass bracelet or necklace chain
- chain-nose pliers
- permanent marker
- old coins, 7
- center punch or nail and hammer
- drill and 1/16" (2mm) bit
- scrap wood for drilling
- round-nose pliers
- 24-gauge sterling silver wire
- wire cutters
- 1 brass toggle clasp (if you aren't using a bracelet that already has a clasp)
- liver of sulfur
- chamois cloth

→ STRESS-AWAY TEA

- peppermint leaves
- French lavender

Blend 2 parts peppermint to one part lavender. Mix it well, thinking only good thoughts of health, wealth and wisdom and prosperity. Add boiling water, let steep for four minutes. Then sip away the stress.

1 If you are using a chain from an old necklace, measure your wrist to determine the length of chain you would like for your bracelet to fit comfortably. You can use pliers to open the links of a premade chain, just as you would a jump ring.

2 Using a permanent marker, mark a drilling hole on each of the coins.

3 Using a center punch or nail and hammer, make an indentation at the marked dot on the coins. Drill a hole at the indentation on each coin.

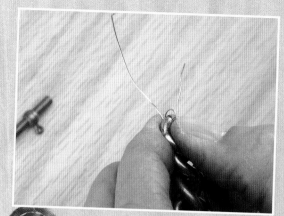

4 Wire wrap the coins to the chain, using round-nose pliers. The coins don't need to be spaced evenly, just eyeball their spacing along the length of the chain.

5 Cut a length of wire to attach the first half of the clasp to one end of the chain. Wrap the wire around the link twice before creating the loop that will hold the clasp.

6 Repeat for the other half of the clasp at the other end of the chain. Patina the bracelet using liver of sulfur, until the desired amount of aging appears. Polish, as desired.

January 6, 1925

Today I received a letter from Francesca. She is on her way to financial recovery. She wrote how she gave away some of her things at first as a way to declutter, but then it felt so good that she gave more away. She went on to say that not soon after, she found new work, earning much more than she was previously. She has been able to pay down her debts, and anticipates being able to be debt free in a year! She went on to say, "This abundance and gratitude thinking really does work!" She said her postcards are coming true, and she will be sending some postcards my way with a thank you.

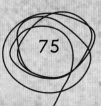

BEAUTY WAY NECKLACE

October 12, 1924

A woman named Ruby came by today. She was agitated at first with a scowl on her face. I had to take deep slow breaths around her so that I, too, would not pick up that prickly nature of hers, and get pulled into her vortex of bitterness. I told her that I knew how to help her, but that she would need to take an active part in her treatment. She felt that I should just heal her and she should just receive. I told her that all healing is a partnership; that if you don't take part you don't heal. It is a natural law.

I told her to drink the Beauty Way Blend morning and evening. I told her to take the necklace I would create and wear it for a month. Each time she put it on or took it off, she was to repeat the Beauty Way Prayer. Then I told her to think of something beautiful that had happened during her day, in her dreams or simply a beautiful thought. Then I told her to perform an act of beauty every day—particularly whenever a negative thought entered her mind, or she felt some of her old bitterness returning.

❧ Intention ❧
I feel the beauty way guiding my life in every way.

Materials and why I chose them:
Mother-of-pearl—purity, innocence, seeing beauty through the eyes of a child
Flowers—beauty
Brass—strength of the sun
Rhinestones—light, radiance

WHAT YOU NEED

- detail brush
- acrylic paints
- 30mm x 20mm mother-of-pearl cabochon
- pencil (optional)
- epoxy glue (E-6000)
- squeeze clamp
- 30mm x 20mm bezel
- jewelry glaze (Diamond Glaze)
- toothpick
- channel cross
- rhinestones, 2ss (or size to fit your cross)
- brass chain
- tin snips or metal shears
- jump rings
- round-nose pliers
- chain-nose pliers
- rhinestone clasp
- brass chain with crystals
- 24-gauge brass wire
- rhinestone beads, 4
- pearls, 2

1 Using a detail brush and acrylic paint, paint a flower motif on the mother-of-pearl cabochon.

2 The tip of a pencil can be used to create tiny dots as flowers or leaves, if that is easier for you than using a brush.

3 Let the paint dry for 24 hours. Glaze the piece and let the glaze dry for 24 hours. Glue the cabochon onto the bezel. Clamp the pieces together and allow 24 hours for the epoxy to cure.

4 Using a toothpick, apply epoxy to the channel cross.

5 Add 2ss rhinestones into the epoxy in the channel cross. Let cure overnight.

6 To begin constructing the chain, cut the plain brass chain into smaller sections, and, using jump rings, reconnect them together with rhinestone beads between them. Try to end up with about a 14" (36cm) chain. Repeat the Beauty Way Prayer as you construct the necklace.

✦ BEAUTY WAY PRAYER

Beauty before me
Beauty behind me
Beauty above me
Beauty below me
Beauty surrounds me, all the days of my life
There is beauty inherently in everything

✦ BEAUTY WAY TEA BLEND

❦ 1 part rose petals
❦ 1 part hibiscus flowers
❦ 1 part borage flowers
❦ 1 part chamomile flowers

❦ 1 part rose hips

Pour boiling water over bouquet, and let steep 5 minutes.
Drink over ice.

7 Wire wrap a final rhinestone onto each end of the chain.

8 Wire wrap this onto one half of the rhinestone clasp.

 9 On the two ends of the crystal chain, begin a wire wrap and on the wire, thread a rhinestone bead, a pearl and a second rhinestone bead.

10 Wire wrap the crystal chain to the other half of the rhinestone clasp.

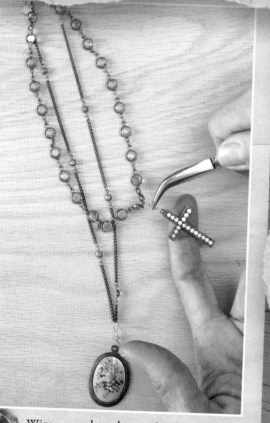

11 Wire wrap the other ends of the chains to the two halves of the rhinestone clasp as well. Finally, wire wrap the cross to the center of the crystal chain and the painted bezel to the center of the plain chain with rhinestones.

November 15, 1924

Today I received a letter from a woman I helped through the Beauty Way. The envelope was decorated in watercolor flowers. I opened it up to find a rather large check to be used in my healing practice. Rose petals fell out with the letter.

The letter said how much she appreciated my kindness, and how everything I told her to do totally transformed her life from one of bitterness and malaise to one of sharing the Beauty Way. She went on to say that she now spreads love and beauty with her work in hospitals, teaching watercolor to the patients. She was so glad to be seeing beauty again and to finally be able to share it with others.

This is why I do what I do.

SELF-LOVE NECKLACE

October 23, 1924

A dear friend asked me today if I might
please make her a talisman to help her
find the strength to love herself once
again. She has felt so much self-loathing
that it is disabling her. Oh how my heart
went out to her. We have all felt this way
at times. So yes, my dear sweet friend, I
will make you a necklace of self-love!

⇒ Intention ⇐

I call upon the good
energies that surround us
everyday, and to release
those energies that are
outmoded and stuck.

Materials and why I chose them:
Copper—conductor of energy
Heart—love
Stamping—a way to use personal symbols
by thinking of the person and the shapes or
symbols that come to mind

October 27, 1924

She was so sad, and the tear streaks that ran down her face from many previous cries showed that she had endured suffering for an extended time. You could see under all of that heaviness a sparkle of what she was, but it was dim. You could feel her sadness in your bones. Everything about her felt heavy and tired. It seemed she took on the world's pain and it was just too much for one person to handle. First, I made up some Uplifting Spirits Tea for her.

I told her to make a wailing wall, similar to the one in Jerusalem—a stacked rock wall. I told her with every rock she stacked to place one of the many burdens she carried into the rock. After she had completed the wall, she was to put on paper any of the other burdens that came to her and to take those papers and stick them between the stones in the wall. If she noticed others that needed her wailing wall, she could invite them over to put their troubles into the wall, too. It would act as a cleansing agent for her and for those who used it. No longer would she carry the weight of the world on her shoulders, but she could hand it over to the strength of the wall.

Lastly, I told her to go for a walk. Walking is good for the soul. It would be good if she takes a daily walk and sees the beauty around her everywhere. During one of those walks, she needs to look for a special stone—whichever stone speaks to her. If she will give me that rock, I will create a necklace for her to keep future burdens at bay.

WHAT YOU NEED

- special rock (or two)
- piece of fabric
- paper that speaks to you: dictionary definitions, quotes, newspaper headings or stories
- acrylic matte medium
- brush
- permanent marker
- glaze—matte or glossy, or shellac
- 18-gauge sterling silver wire
- round-nose pliers
- wire cutters
- 1mm leather cord
- needle-nose pliers
- epoxy (E-6000)
- spring clips, 2

UPLIFTING SPIRITS TEA

- dried peach slices
- dried apricot slices
- blend of hibiscus and black tea leaves

Mix all together and steep in hot water for 3 minutes. Pour over ice.

Intention

With each rock I hold and decorate, may I remember that worry, sadness and fear can always be replaced back into the earth to be cleansed and renewed.

Materials and why I chose them:
Rocks—bones of the earth, can carry and transform our burdens
Sterling silver—innate power
Copper—conductor of energy

85

 Select your rock(s). I look for heart-shaped rocks to remind that love conquers all. Lay the rock(s) on a piece of fabric so they stand out.

 Cut out pieces of magazines, use decorative paper, old letters or fabric—anything that symbolizes what you are feeling and what you want to release. Think of your heaviness; what does it look like? Once you have gathered enough to represent your burden, you are ready to collage your rock(s). Apply acrylic matte medium to the pieces of your collage, and adhere them to the rock.

3 Coat with additional medium. Work on it until it feels right.

4 Add details or symbols, using a permanent marker.

5 Glaze or shellac over the whole rock to seal it.

6 Working off the spool of 18-gauge wire, use a pair of round-nose pliers to begin a cage for your rock. Start with a small loop at the end of the wire.

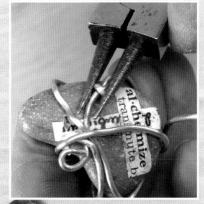

 7 Positioning the loop at the top of the rock, wrap the wire around the rock by going up and down the rock vertically and wrapping around the initial loop to secure it. Trim the excess wire and crimp the last loop with the pliers.

 8 Thread the end of the wire from the spool through the wire on the rock and create a new loop at the end.

 9 Now go horizontally around the rock, and continue wrapping so that you create a cage—you are caging these heavy thoughts.

 10 When you feel the rock is sufficiently wrapped, cut the wire and use the round-nose pliers to help tuck the wire tail under a wrap.

11 Cut three 24" (61cm) pieces of leather cord. Hold the three cords together and knot them together. Begin braiding the leather. When you reach what you consider to be the halfway point of the necklace, slip the caged rock onto one of the leather cords.

 12 Continue braiding. When you reach the end of the braid, secure the strands temporarily by tying a second knot.

 13 Check the fit of the necklace around your neck, the heart rock should land over your heart. Make two wire hooks from 18-gauge wire. Remove one of the knots and braid in a wire hook.

 14 Retie the knot, using a pair of needle-nose pliers to pull the knot tight.

 15 Add a bit of epoxy to the knot.

 16 Repeat steps 13–15 to add the remaining hook. Clamp the knots with spring clips and let the epoxy cure.

This necklace should be worn until the heart has released the heavy feelings into the rock. After the wearer can feel the release, they should remove the rock necklace and either uncage it and place the rock in the Wailing Wall, bury it or put it in a bowl as a reminder of all that was released.

November 30, 1924

I received a postcard from the lady with the wailing wall. At least twelve people have inserted paper into her wall. The woman wrote that people have found her wall to be extremely comforting and it has brought healing, forgiveness and comfort to many.

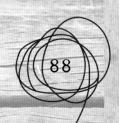

TWELVE-STEP NECKLACE OF NEW BEGINNINGS

WHAT YOU NEED

- permanent marker
- 18-gauge copper sheet
- tin snips
- sandpaper
- assorted metal stamps
- hammer
- steel bench block
- two-hole punch or $\frac{1}{16}$" (2mm) punch
- 20-gauge sterling silver wire
- round-nose pliers
- 1" (3cm) brass disks, 2
- $\frac{3}{4}$" (19mm) sterling silver disks, 2
- beads (optional)
- handmade hook clasp (see page 20)
- liver of sulfur

October 29, 1924

Today was a drizzly sort of day—a gentle cleansing rain on the eve of a new moon—a nourishing rain of the desert.

My next guest will need a cleansing of her own—a new start. She was a very pretty girl, but she was bloated in the midsection from alcohol. You can tell because alcoholics look pickled, and she definitely looked pickled. She looked disheveled, and she reeked of alcohol. I told her she must come back sober; I do not work with people who are not sober.

89

❧ Intention ❧

One step at a time, one day at a time, life can become better and better. . . .

Materials and why I chose them:
Crosses—strength, direction, four corners, four seasons, four periods of the day, crossroads and journeys

→ STEPS TO RECOVERY

1. Find your power within.
2. Know that you are protected.
3. Know that if you listen within you will find your answers.
4. Look in the mirror and remind yourself you are perfect, and you will be perfection today.
5. Know that you can do it today, and worry only about today.
6. Look in the mirror and repeat "I believe in myself."
7. Do a chore you don't like today.
8. Watch the sunset and congratulate yourself for being free from addictions today.
9. Remember that life is lived one small step at a time.
10. Take a moral inventory.
11. Remember your dreams today, and take a step toward them. Any step.
12. To every negative, make something positive happen whether it be in thought or deed.

1 Draw your desired shape of a cross onto the sheet metal, using a permanent marker. Using tin snips, cut out the cross.

2 Using sandpaper, sand the cross to remove any remaining marker and to polish the metal.

3 Add texture to the cross using stamps or other tools and a hammer.

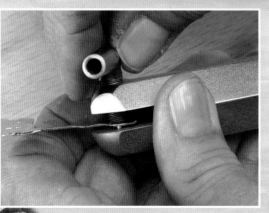

4 Punch a hole at the top of the cross, using a two-hole punch or a hammer and a $\frac{1}{16}$" (2mm) punch.

5 Wire wrap the cross to the center of the chain, using silver wire and the jewelry pliers.

6 Attach all the crosses and charms by wire wrapping them onto the chain. Add beads to some of the wraps as you see fit.

7 The chain can be broken up with wraps of beads if you like.

8 Attach your clasp to the ends of the chain.

Note: Be sure to add a patina to this piece. As the wearer handles it and wears it, the natural polishing that will occur can signify the cleansing and rebirth of the person's life.

After presenting her with the finished necklace, I told my client that each morning and evening she was to review her recovery steps. Every evening, instead of a drink, she is to make herself a chamomile seltzer. This will relax her and prevent further depletion of her body. It will also help her with her digestion. She can also drink chamomile tea with a hint of fresh-squeezed lemon juice in the morning. Her system needs to be cleansed.

Lastly, I want her to write a story for herself—how she perceives her new life—what she expects from it and how she is going to live it. I want her to write down several steps towards her new life. Then, each day, along with her recovery program, she will read and review her story. Each day she will take a step, no excuses.

Each cross in this necklace represents a step in her program and new life beginnings.

January 8, 1925

I just received word from a client I'd helped with a recovery plan three months ago. She wrote to tell me she was alcohol free, that she has a new job with a salary she felt she was worth. She is finally getting paid her dream salary.

February 12, 1925

I just received another letter from my recovered client. She has met the man of her dreams and she is still alcohol free! One step, one cross, one month at a time.

CIRCLE-OF-ANGER NECKLACE AND RING

October 30, 1924

I was up all night with an angry thunderstorm. It was fast and furious. This morning, a small drizzle, but I could sleep no longer. When the thunder awoke me at 4AM, I could feel the static in the air. It will be a hot day today. In heat, anger arises. . . . I am meeting someone today with anger issues. I shall make some Cooling Tempers Tea.

At 3PM, just as the sun was close to being the hottest in the desert, my next guest arrived. He had a scowl and walked fiercely. He admitted he got angry a lot. He said he felt so bottled up most of the time and just felt as if he would burst like a volcano (and often did). He realized he was hurting others but felt he had no control.

⇢ Intention ⇠

I release my anger to the winds to dissipate it, and I release my anger into the rocks to be free.

Materials and why I chose them:
Silver—innate power
Rocks—carry our burdens without objections
Oval—containment and rebirth, an egg of new beginnings

→ COOLING TEMPERS TEA

- 1 part spearmint, picked on the full moon
- 1 part peppermint, picked on the full moon
- A pinch of lavender buds, gathered when they reach full bloom

Mix them together and steep, thinking cooling and happy thoughts.

WHAT YOU NEED

- permanent marker
- template of an oval, about 2" x 1½" (5cm x 4cm)
- 18-gauge sterling silver sheet
- tin snips or jeweler's saw
- file
- sandpaper
- hammer (or, ideally, stones)
- steel bench block
- dapping block and dap or a stone to shape the disk
- two-hole punch or ¹⁄₁₆" (2mm) punch
- leather cord
- chain-nose pliers
- 24-gauge sterling silver wire
- ring mandrel or appropriately sized dowel
- leather mallet or rubber mallet

1 Using a permanent marker, trace the oval template on silver sheet. Cut out the shape with tin snips or a jeweler's saw. Create two ovals.

2 File the edges to remove any burrs and to smooth them.

93

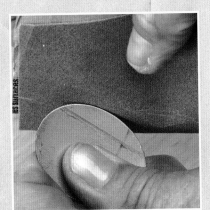

3 Sand the disks using sandpaper.

4 Release anger into the oval disks by hammering your anger with the stones onto the steel bench block. With each stroke, release a past knot of frustration or anger.

5 Using a dap and dapping block, dome each disk to the desired shape.

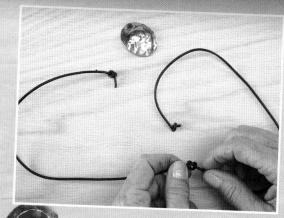

6 Again, file any rough edges. Punch a hole in the top of the disk that is to be the pendant, using a two-hole punch or a hammer and a ¹⁄₁₆" (2mm) punch.

7 Cut a length of leather cord 16"–18" (41cm–46cm). Tie a knot in the center of the cord.

8 Using jewelry pliers, create a wire wrap through the hole on the disk and run one tail of the wire through the knot on the cord.

Note: Knot the ends of the leather thong, and tie around your neck. When the necklace falls off, a part of your anger has fallen away. Keep putting the necklace back on until you feel you have control of your anger.

9 For the ring, form the other disk around a ring mandrel or a dowel, shaping it with your hands.

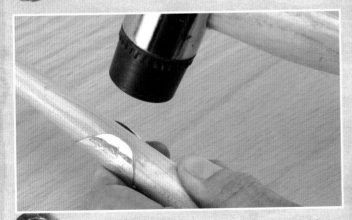

10 Refine the round shape, using a leather or rubber mallet.

Note: Wear the ring on your index finger to direct your anger, or on your middle finger to control your anger. You no longer need to wear it once your anger is under control, but you may as a gentle reminder.

I had him hammer his anger into this disk using stones. Copper and silver are good conductors so it will take the anger and ground it into the second stone. Stones are the bones of the earth and they will ground the negative energy.

I instructed him to eat often, as low blood sugar will trigger anger. I told him to carry a few almonds in his pocket for a quick protein snack to ensure his sugar levels remain balanced. Lastly, I told him to try to take time to be grateful and to see the beauty around him daily.

I told him to say a prayer intending the disk to remind him what his anger can do to others and himself. Let it be a reminder that signifies the release of anger.

December 1, 1924

Today I received a call from the once-angry man. He told me he was doing great, that people admire his disks often, and he tells them the story about Inspiritu. He said he has new relations with his family, for which he is grateful. He said he started to make hammered steel sculptures after his visit here, and he is sending me one. He has even managed to start selling some of them! Well, goes to show you what a little release can do. . . .

REMEMBRANCE NECKLACE

October 31, 1924

Day of the Dead is a time of remembering our ancestors. This is a special celebration in my world. In addition to honoring our loved ones, we burn what is no longer useful—resentments, angers, petty jealousies. We bury our resentments, and we feed those memories close to us. Today Rosita came to me with a medal her father had given her as a child. As he had passed away, she wanted a special necklace to wear for the Dia de los Muertos celebration in her town tonight. I told her I would work on it right away.

⇾ Intention ⇽

I honor those before me. I praise those who showed me the way, and I release all that is no longer useful, healthy or wise.

Materials and why I chose them:
Brass—strength of the sun
Charm or medal of significance—a reminder of the original bearer
Flower filigree—beauty we shared with the ones we have left behind

WHAT YOU NEED

- ruler
- piece of leather at least 24" x 1" (61cm x 3cm)
- permanent marker
- scissors
- jeweler's glue or epoxy (E-6000)
- brass end caps for ½" (13mm) ribbon, 2
- chain-nose pliers
- spring clamps, 2
- awl
- 24-gauge sterling silver wire
- silk thread ball beads, 2
- filigree gold ball beads, 2
- round-nose pliers
- fabric hardener and paint-brush
- lace trim
- liver of sulfur
- flower filigree
- square filigree
- special coin or medal for the back of the piece
- special medallion or medal given to you by the one you choose to remember

1 Using a ruler that is approximately 1" (3cm) wide, mark down both sides of the ruler with a marker, for the length of 22" (56cm).

2 Find the center between the two marked lines and make marks down the length of the leather to divide it in half.

3 Using scissors, cut out the wide strip of leather, and then cut along the marked line that divides the length in half to create two 22" (56cm) strips.

 4 Apply jeweler's glue or epoxy to the inside of one end cap. Press the leather strip into the cap and squeeze it shut using pliers.

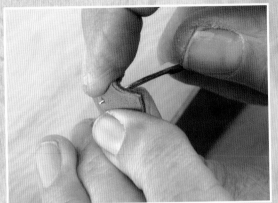

5 Clamp the piece tightly and let the epoxy cure. Repeat for the other side. Using the awl or a pair of sharp pointed scissors, poke a hole at the raw end of one strip.

 6 Using 24-gauge wire, create a rosary wrap (see page 18) with a silk thread ball.

7 Create a rosary wrap with a filigree bead, connecting it to the silk thread ball on one end and the hole in the end of the leather on the other end. Repeat on the other strap.

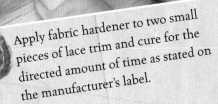

8 Apply fabric hardener to two small pieces of lace trim and cure for the directed amount of time as stated on the manufacturer's label.

9 Using round-nose pliers, wire wrap one lace piece to the end cap on one of the straps.

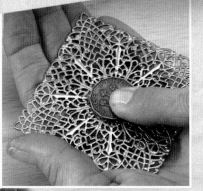

10 Repeat for the other piece of hardened lace. Patina the brass pieces with liver of sulfur. Using epoxy, glue the filigree flower to the large filigree square. Glue the special coin to the back of the piece.

11 Glue the medal over the coin. Clamp all of the pieces together and wait 24 hours or so for the epoxy to cure.

12 Using jewelry pliers, wire wrap the large filigree square to the lace pieces using two pieces of sterling silver wire for each piece of lace.

Note: This is a great way to remember those you love by incorporating something special they had once given you into a necklace that can be worn as a form of remembrance, a reminder of their love.

.11080

99

FOCUS PRAYER STRAND

November 5, 1924

My next client appeared as if she were flittering like a butterfly on a hot summer day, checking out all the beautiful flowers, but not knowing where to land. As she sat, I noticed her leg moving back and forth as if keeping rhythm to some unknown time. She kept moving around in her seat as if she were uncomfortable sitting still, which I gather she was. She was tiring me out just watching her.

She is here because she needs my help to slow down and focus. It seems that mind of hers never stops jumping around from one thought to the next. I brought her some of my famous Focus Tea.

⇾ Intention ⇽

May I remember as I focus on each bead, and repeat my power phrase or word, that it is one prayer, one bead and one step at a time.

Materials and why I chose them:
Silver—innate power
Charms, beads and colors—each bead and charm was chosen for its focusing properties

→ FOCUS TEA

- cinnamon
- black tea leaves
- green tea leaves
- cardamom
- ginger
- freshly ground black pepper

Mix equal parts of the above, along with any other secret ingredients you feel help you focus. Add a pinch of a focus prayer and let steep. Serve warm.

I explained to her that she has been given the gift of enthusiasm, but that left unchecked, it leads to lack of focus and burnout in the long run. Our gift of energy needs to be harnessed. I told her to drink the tea for three days, to come back after that period and I would have what she needed then.

WHAT YOU NEED

- small medallions and talismans that are reminders to focus
- 20-gauge sterling silver wire
- round-nose pliers
- sword charm (to destroy wrong thoughts, wrong deeds, temptations and impulses that lead you away from focus)
- pig charm (to remind you when you are being piggish or over-indulging your senses)
- 19-strand steel beading wire
- crimp tubes, 4
- pendulum
- crimping pliers
- beads of any shape and color, about 100 or so
- jump rings
- large silver ring

1 Wrap medallions or other talismans that don't have preexisting stringing holes with 20-gauge wire. Wrap in a cage style (see page 86–87), creating loops at the top to hang from. Gather additional charms, including a sword and a pig as well.

2 Cut about 40" (102cm) of stringing wire. At one end, string on two crimp tubes. String the wire through the bail on the pendulum, and then back through the crimp tubes. Use the crimping pliers to close the crimp tubes, leaving the tail wire intact.

3 Randomly begin stringing on the beads. When you feel like it, add a wire wrapped charm or talisman. Charms may be threaded with a jump ring and added that way, too.

4 As you add on various beads and charms, say a prayer over each for focus and reminders of focus. Add the sword charm with the intention of slicing through unnecessary actions and time wasters.

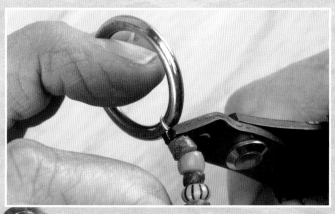

5 For the pig charm, say a prayer that the pig will remind you when you are being piggish and hoarding. Continue to add the beads onto the focus necklace until all beads are on the necklace. When all 108 beads have been added, string on the remaining two crimp tubes. String the wire through the large silver ring and back through the crimp tubes, as well as a few beads. Pull the wire taut and crimp the tubes with the crimping pliers.

6 Wrap the ends of the strand with a bit of silver wire to hide the crimp tubes and create a more finished look.

Note: The finished strand can be wrapped around the shoulders like a shawl, allowing the wearer to be "surrounded by focus." The pendulum of this strand can also act as a divining tool. Ask a question, and allow the necklace to hang straight with the pendulum pointing down. If the pendulum swings from side to side, the answer is yes. If it doesn't move, there is no answer at this time. If it swings top to bottom, the answer is no.

To use the strand as you would a string of prayer beads, first choose a holy name or word that means something to you. Use only one word and use that same word the entire time when you are working through your focus strand. Say the holy name or word at each bead as your fingers walk along the strand.

When you get to a charm, affirm that you will overcome all obstacles associated with that charm. Soon you will see great improvement in your entire being, as you become more focused, centered and balanced. Use the charms to instill within yourself those traits you wish to see manifested.

November 19, 1924

It's now been two weeks since I completed the girl's focus strand, and rumor has it that she has since taken steps to start her own company. She will be the owner of a natural perfumery. I suspect her favorite scent will resemble Focus Tea. . . .

NO-FEAR TRAVEL BRACELET

November 12, 1924

His head was darting to and fro, like caged animal, eyes wide. I could sense he was petrified. He explained to me he was scared to death of traveling and of meeting new people. He was scared he would panic and that something would happen. It has been like being in jail. I told him that I could help him and I made him some Peace of Mind Tea.

The dream pillow would calm him when he felt panic coming on. I told him to breathe into the pillow deeply and slow his breath by focusing on his inhale and exhale.

St. Christopher is the patron saint of travelers; the coral beads are for healing and to keep his blood moving so he is never stagnant in fear again. When people are fearful, it is best to work the fingers around beads, repeating a sacred name or a holy word. On the medal for courage, a prayer of peace within. I told him to keep it on his wrist, or in his pocket for easy access.

103

WHAT YOU NEED

- coral beads, 21
- elastic cord
- scissors
- small squares of fabric, 2
- needle and thread
- dried chamomile (a tea bag will work)
- sterling silver jump ring
- thin satin ribbon
- 24-gauge sterling silver wire
- round-nose pliers
- St. Christopher's medal for travelers
- military medal for courage
- turquoise stone
- chain-nose pliers

≫ Intention ≪

Fear is love reversed. There is no fear in love.

Materials and why I chose them:
Coral—protection
Chamomile—calming properties
Lavender—calming properties
Saint Christopher—medal for travelers

→ PEACE OF MIND TEA

- hibiscus flowers
- rose petals
- chamomile flowers

Mix equal parts of the three flowers. Pour boiling water over the top and let steep for 2-3 minutes. Pour over ice and sit back and allow the tea to penetrate your mind and relax your body.

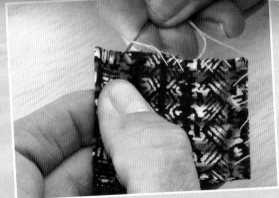

 1 Rub the beads in your hands until they gather heat and life force. Concentrate on the healing energy (love, protection and the release of fear) coming through your hands into the beads. String the coral beads onto the elastic. Make two double loop knots and trim the excess elastic cord.

 2 Cut two squares of fabric to 1½" (4cm). Using the needle and thread, with right sides facing one another, sew together three sides.

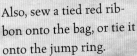

3 Turn right-side out and stuff the small pillow with dried lavender and chamomile.

4 Sew up the open side. Sew on a jump ring to one corner of the pillow.

5 Also, sew a tied red ribbon onto the bag, or tie it onto the jump ring.

6 Using sterling silver wire and round-nose pliers, wire wrap St. Christopher's medal onto the strand, and state that it is providing protection. Wire wrap the military medal for courage and also the turquoise stone by looping the wire around the stone as a cage first (see page 86–87).

7 Using both the pliers to open and close the jump ring, add the fabric pillow to the bracelet, opposite the medals.
Note: End with the statement that "Courage, peace and protection follow [individual] all the days of his/her life."

April 15, 1925

I just received a letter from the once-fearful traveler. He now has an import/export business and travels all over the world. He has many foreign offices, and would be glad to source anything I might need. So much for fear!

PRECIOUS TIME NECKLACE

November 15, 1924

Today I had a client come to me, frantic about time. She said she had very little. I asked her what she meant. She said there is so much to do but not enough time to do it. I told her that if we are using it wisely, it seems to expand, but if we chase it, it seems to run away. She told me she hadn't thought that way before. So I made her this Precious Time Necklace to remind her to use her time wisely.

➤ Intention ➤

I live, work and love in the precious present.

Materials and why I chose them:

Silver—innate power

Clock—time

Silver rosary chain—moments that click away when we are not present or in communion with life

Medals—goodness inherent in the present moment

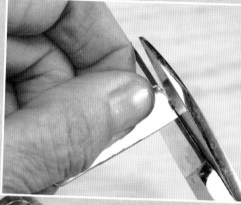

 1 To make your own bail, cut out a ½" x 1" (13mm x 3cm) rectangle from the sterling silver sheet, using tin snips.

 2 Using the hammer, bench block and stamps, decorate the metal strip.

WHAT YOU NEED

- 18-gauge sterling silver sheet
- tin snips
- hammer
- steel bench block
- decorative metal stamps
- liver of sulfur
- round-nose pliers
- old watch face
- old silver rosary chain
- 14" (36cm) sterling silver chain, 2
- rhinestone clasp
- small medals, 2
- medal of your favorite saint (I chose Joan of Arc for her stick-to-it attitude)
- 24-gauge sterling silver wire
- filigree pin
- chain-nose pliers

 3 Patina and polish the bail. Using round-nose pliers, coil under one end of the strip. Thread the pin of the watch face through the coil, then squeeze it shut using pliers.

4 Clip the Y-portion off of the rosary chain.

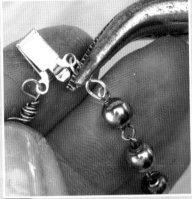

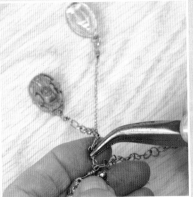

5 Cut 2" (5cm) from each of the 14" (36cm) chains. Wire wrap one end of the rosary chain and one of the 12" (30cm) chains to one half of the rhinestone clasp using the round-nose pliers.

6 Wire wrap the other end of the rosary chain and the other 12" (30cm) chain to the other half of the rhinestone clasp. Wire wrap the medals onto the two pieces of 2" (5cm) chain and wire wrap them onto the rhinestone clasp (either half).

7 Wire wrap the Joan of Arc medal to the center of the rosary chain.

8 Attach one corner of the filigree pin to each of the 12" (30cm) sterling silver chains, using chain-nose pliers.

9 At the bottom of the filigree pin, wire wrap the bail of the watch face.
Set the watch face to a time when you feel most energized, most tranquil, whatever hour of the day seems to be your best. What is your magical hour?

BROKEN HEART NECKLACE

November 21, 1924

I had to drive to visit a client at their home today. I was told of a young person who would not leave her family's ranch and was despondent. I drove nearly two hours through the mountainous terrain and desert scrub. I drove down the rocky, bumpy road for two miles, and there in the distance was the ranch house. Just as I pulled up, the mother greeted me at the car. The girl had a sunken, apathetic expression, slow moves and just seemingly dead to everything around her.

→ MENDING A BROKEN HEART TEA

- rose petals
- rose hips
- rose buds
- linden flowers
- lemongrass herbs
- lemon verbena
- chamomile
- oat straw

Mix all ingredients and set in a small strainer, balanced on the top of a cup. Pour in boiling water and let steep to the companion-call songs of the birds. Pour over ice or drink hot. Drink morning and night or as much as needed.

I was told the girl had come home, about a week ago, crying and inconsolable. It turns out her friend had had convulsions at school and they had to take him to the hospital. That night she got a call, and his parents explained that he had died in the hospital. That is when she had shut down. He was her first love. It seems no one could help her out of her despondency, or even raise any sort of emotion from her. She seemed to have lost her will to live.

≫ Intention ≪

May I remember that it is in loving that one is loved.

Materials and why I chose them:
Miraculous medals—love, protection, miracles
Sterling silver—innate power
Turquoise heart—healing
Bird charm—love birds
Rhinestone—light and radiance
Sacred heart—love

WHAT YOU NEED

- miraculous medal (such as a saint medallion or any meaningful Milagros)
- 3" (8cm) fine found sterling chain
- 24-gauge sterling wire
- 5" (13m) medium found sterling chain, 2pcs
- small bead
- round-nose pliers
- 16-gauge wire
- hammer
- steel bench block
- chain-nose pliers
- double-bird charm
- heart-shaped turquoise stone
- rhinestone shoe clip or necklace piece

1 Wire wrap the miraculous medal to the 3" (8cm) chain.

2 Wire wrap the chain to one of the 5" (13cm) pieces of chain, adding a bead to the connector.

3 With the round-nose pliers create a U-shape in 16-gauge wire, with small loops on the ends. Hammer the U-shape flat for strength. Repeat with a second piece of wire, making the U a bit lopsided. This second piece will act as the hook. Using jewelry pliers, wire wrap one half of the clasp near the place you connected the smaller chain. Wire wrap the hook half to the other piece of 5" (13cm) chain using jewelry pliers.

4 Wire wrap the double-bird charm onto the turquoise heart, then wire wrap the rhinestone shoe clip onto the other half of the connection wrap.

5 Wire wrap one half of the chain to the rhinestone shoe clip, about one-third of the way in, using jewelry pliers. Repeat on the other side of the shoe clip, with the other half of the chain.

December 23, 1924

I just got a call from the girl at the ranch. She wanted me to know that she had formed a group at school called the Lonely Hearts Club. It is a club for those that have lost someone or that felt lost. The club volunteers at hospitals, nursing homes and anywhere else they are needed to share and care. They bake cookies, read stories, but most of all they just share beauty and companionship. Yes, she said everything is great in her life. She even has a new boyfriend.

QUOTE-OF-INSPIRATION NECKLACE

December 7, 1924

It is a blustery day. The dust devils are twirling furiously. Everything seems to be in twisted motion. It is a day in need of centering.

My client today is a writer, and it is so strange that she traveled here amidst all of this turmoil. She explained to me that turmoil and inner doubt are blocking her writing abilities. I knew just the antidote.

I told her, in order for the piece I was about to make to work, she needed to find her most inspiring quote and write it on a small sheet of paper.

❧ Intention ❧

May I remember to be surprised; to wonder is to finally understand.

Materials and why I chose them:

Book—beauty of the written word
Silver—innate power
Rhinestones—light
Rosary chain—memorize quote one bead at a time

WHAT YOU NEED

- rose links, 6
- round-nose pliers
- 24-gauge sterling silver wire
- various sterling silver chains, 3
- jump ring
- rosary chain
- meaningful medals, links or charms, 3
- liver of sulfur
- book-locket or rosary case
- paper to write your quote on
- scissors
- jewelry glue
- rhinestone clasp
- needle-nose pliers

1 Connect three rose links together with wire wraps using round-nose pliers and 24-gauge silver wire. Select one sterling silver chain and wire wrap a long enough length of it to the three connected rose links to make an 8" (20cm) length. Repeat for the other three rose links and a matching length of chain. Attach a wire wrap loop to the rose links on the ends of each length so you can connect them with a jump ring. Thread a jump ring through the two loops and through the bail of the locket. Close the jump ring with pliers.

2 With your rosary chain and your remaining sterling silver chains, create a total of three more chain lengths—mixing and matching sections if you like. Also include your chosen medals and/or charms in the mix. Create one chain that is 15½" (39cm), one that is 14" (36cm) and one that is 13" (33cm). With the locket chain, you should now have four pieces.

3 Patina all the metal pieces you want aged. Select a quote for your locket. There are a ton of resources for finding quotes, including the Internet. Find the one that strikes a beat with your heart. That is the one you need at this moment.

Hand write the quote or print it from your computer, then trim it to a size that, when folded, will fit in your locket. Here, my quote is on a ½" x 5" (13mm x 13cm) strip. Fold your quote accordion-style and, using jewelry glue, attach one end of it to the inside of your locket. (Or, if you think you will want to switch out your quote from time to time, just set it in loose—no glue needed.)

4 Keeping the chains aligned, longest to shortest, wire wrap the ends of the four chains to one half of the rhinestone clasp.

5 Without twisting the chains or changing their order, attach the other ends of the chains to the other half of the clasp. Finish off the piece with a medal wire wrapped to a 2" (5cm) piece of chain and wire wrap it to the last link on one of the chains, near the clasp.

FIND-YOUR-VOICE CUFF BRACELET

December 15, 1924

Olivia, a client of mine, came by today. She could barely speak, and was bent over like a Mexican Elder tree. She felt off balance and that she wasn't being heard.

I asked her why she felt this way. She said her husband doesn't listen to her. He constantly beats her down in word and deed and rarely has a compliment. She feels she can do no right. It's as if the people around her are constantly finding fault in all she does.

I told her that each time she felt she was being nitpicked, condemned, corrected or found faulty to take a deep breath and send that person love. Tighten your stomach to gain inner power and ground yourself using the golden light of healing. Continue to praise the person correcting you with the opposite of what they are criticizing you for. Release the breath. If you still feel tense, breathe in, hold it and breathe out slowly. This breath is very calming.

I told her to remember that those that are most critical and judgmental are more so to themselves. They have little self-worth as they must constantly criticize others to make themselves feel superior.

I told her to work with the affirmation and the breath. I also told her that we would make her a cuff bracelet to help her find her voice.

❧ Intention ❧

I may breathe in what life has to offer, but I can as easily exhale that which does not serve my needs.

Materials and why I chose them:

Copper—conductor of energy

WHAT YOU NEED

- 18-gauge copper sheet
- tin snips or metal shears
- center punch
- scrap wood
- drill and $1/8$" (3mm) bit
- rubber stamp(s)
- permanent ink stamp pad or permanent marker
- duct tape
- etchant solution
- plastic container
- paper towels
- bracelet mandrel or similar round object such as a can
- rubber mallet
- $2\frac{1}{2}$" (6cm) lace
- scissors
- needle and thread
- three small buttons

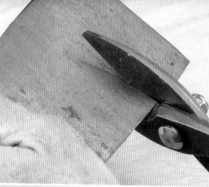

1 From the copper sheet, cut out a 2" x 3" (5cm x 8cm) rectangle, using tin snips or shears.

2 At about ¼" (3mm) in from each side, use the center punch to mark a hole in each corner of the copper. Working on a piece of scrap wood, drill a hole at the mark in each corner.

3 Stamp your desired design/imagery onto the metal using a rubber stamp and an ink such as StazOn or VersaMark, or if you rather, you can freehand something using a permanent marker.

4 Let the ink dry. Place a piece of duct tape onto the back of the copper piece, with at least 2" (5cm) of excess tape on each end. If the tape is not wide enough, apply a second piece.

5 Make sure the tape is thoroughly secured to the back of the copper by rubbing it down with your fingers. Pour some etchant solution into a plastic dish. Submerge the copper piece, stamped side down, into the liquid. Use the excess tape to secure the copper piece.

6 Check the copper piece every half hour until you get the level of etching you desire. Rinse the copper piece in a bath of water to stop the reaction. You can pour the excess etchant liquid into a separate container (that has a lid) to re-use. Do not pour it down the drain. Neutralize it with baking soda and then take it to a waste disposal facility for proper disposal.

7 Using a paper towel, pat dry the copper piece.

8 Working on a bracelet mandrel or a similar curved surface, hammer the etched copper with a rubber mallet to form a curved, cuff shape.

9 Cut a piece of 2½" (6cm) lace to an 8" (20cm) length. Using a needle and thread, hand stitch the copper to the center of the lace.

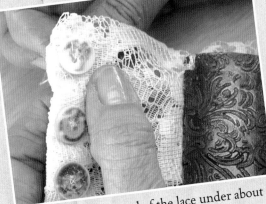

10 Turn one end of the lace under about ½" (13mm) and sew on three buttons.

11 At the other end of the lace, cut three slits where the buttons will go. Sew around the openings with the thread and needle to keep the buttonhole edges from fraying.

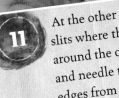

11080

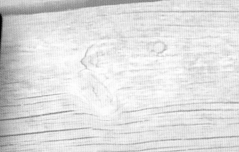

INNER LIGHT NECKLACE

December 21, 1924

Winter solstice—the longest night of the year: a time when Yule logs, as well as great bonfires, were burned to seek light in that darkest time of the year. It is during these dark times—when we feel our lowest—that we need to remember our inner fire, our inner light. It is our inner light that inspired this necklace.

Magdalena came to me on this night of longest nights in hopes I could ignite her inner light. She has had an attack of extreme depression. She said she can barely move; it hurts her too much. I told her that even in the darkest hour there is light burning somewhere to remove the darkness. I told her we would find this light within her together. We will make an inner light necklace to remind her that she carries her inner light within her at all times. We then proceeded to light candles and I added a drop of frankincense and myrrh on top of the burning candles to let the holy scent envelop us and lift us up.

❧ Intention ❧

Even in the darkest hour your inner light shines to guide you.

Materials and why I chose them:

Rhinestones—inner light
Brass—strength of the sun and the light within
Medal—we are perfect as we are

WHAT YOU NEED

- vintage brass chains, 2 types
- vintage rhinestone bracelet
- handmade S hook (see page 20)
- 24-gauge sterling silver wire
- round-nose pliers
- chain-nose pliers
- two-hole metal punch or drill and $^1/_{16}$" (2mm) bit
- old honorable medal

1 Take off the clasps from the vintage components.

2 Wire wrap a 2" (5cm) length of a smaller brass chain to a larger brass chain. My chain came with a small round bead at the end, which I decided to leave intact.

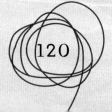

3 Wire wrap one end of the rhinestone bracelet to the S hook, using 24-gauge silver wire and round-nose and chain-nose pliers.

4 Wire wrap the other end of the rhinestone bracelet to the remaining end of the larger brass chain.

5 Using a two-hole metal punch or a drill and ¹⁄₁₆" (2mm) bit, create two holes at the top of the medal.

6 Center the medal under the rhinestone bracelet. Using round-nose pliers and chain-nose pliers, attach the medal to the bracelet with a wire wrap at each hole.

FAREWELL

Time was drawing to a close for my visit at Inspiritu, and my work with Milagros' prescription book. I was a bit sad at the thought. Her kindness and her love of people had truly inspired me as I read through each story of healing. I closed the book and pondered what a special place Inspiritu is—a place of healing and magic. I looked out over the Christmas Mountains with a special cup of tea called Fare Thee Well.

→ FARE THEE WELL TEA

- dried coconut
- loose black tea

Mix the coconut and the black tea well. Mix up enough to make several cups and put in an airtight container. Steep your first cup on a day you wish to remember. Then, after that special day, each time you go to make the tea, shake the container vigorously to release the gentle coconut aroma. Its smell will call you back every time.

As I was about to leave, I saw a pile of old Milagros in the corner of the house. They were patinaed with age. I thought to myself that I would make a Miracle-Thinking Necklace in honor of Milagros and her prescription book of miracle thinking. Each little Milagros will be given away to someone who might need it, and when the necklace has released all of its miracles it will have fulfilled the purpose Milagros had for her prescription book.

WHERE TO GO TO FIND THINGS

Scour flea markets, antique stores, vintage stores, and resale shops; but don't forget to look through grandma's trunks, and jewelry discards from family, friends and clients. Look at the creative possibilities inherent in each piece. Are there gemstones that can be salvaged? Is there a great pendant on a chain, even if you don't like the chain? Does something on the piece grab your attention? Can the piece be repaired or altered? Does looking at the piece draw any sort of emotional reaction from you? Is there an antidote apparent in it? Make sure you keep your prescription book handy to jot down any favorite stores, history of pieces, and any other information that comes your way on your adventures.

Here are some things you might want to look for:

Beads, Gemstones and Baubles: Look for these at bead shows, bead stores, jewelry supply stores, on the Internet, millinery supply stores, wedding gown stores and at lighting stores where they sell crystal chandeliers. Some of my favorites are scuffed sterling silver beads, baroque pearls and odd-shaped pearls, turquoise, gemstones—such as garnets, apatite and carnelian, rhinestone bits and pieces and old millinery flowers.

Jewelry Findings: You can find these on the Internet as well as jewelry supply stores and craft stores. Additionally, look for unusual clasps, buttons, jump rings and closures on vintage jewelry that you find.

Medals and Rosaries: Look at Catholic supply stores, antique stores, vintage stores, some craft stores and on the Internet.

Found Objects: Look everywhere and anywhere for these beauties. You can find some of these items at craft supply stores, import stores, jewelry supply stores and hardware stores. Think of new uses for pieces. Look around your own home! Use your creative thinking cap: bottle caps as reliquary bezels, rosary boxes and lip balm tins for bezels, old bracelets, old rosary bits and pieces, mica, old photos, old holy cards, quotes, cameos and interesting pendants. . . . So many objects have hidden potential, just waiting for you to instill them with meaning.

Patina Solutions and Etching Solutions: These can be found at jewelry supply stores/catalogs, art and craft supply stores and stained glass supply stores. You can also always try the hardboiled egg trick. Leave the piece with a hardboiled egg for a week; if you can stand the stench you will have a perfect patina!

Herbs, Spices and Medicinal Supplies: For the recipes in this book, shea butter, bottles and containers, herbs, spices and dried flowers can be found at ethnic grocery stores, local health food stores, some craft stores, herbal catalogs, spa catalogs and the Internet. Whenever possible, I recommend homegrown and dried herbs and flowers. I also recommend picking the flowers and herbs on a full moon when they are most potent and drying them on screens in the attic (or other warm place) with plenty of airflow. They are even more suited for the recipes given when you prepare them yourself.

123

INDEX

125

MARIE FRENCH
Curandera from a Small Texas Town

Part French, part German, part Irish, Marie has settled into the mountains of far west Texas with her family. It is in amongst the dust devils, cactus and majestic mountains that she learned of the tales of the curanderas. She mixed and stirred the curanderas' recipes and prescriptions together with her own family history of herbal lore, tales and artistic endeavors. Part healing pilgrimage, part compendium of herbal lore and knowledge, this healing jewelry book will surely take your jewelry-making experience to new levels.

Marie French has taught art in schools and workshops, from preschoolers through adults. She has exhibited in galleries, museums and libraries across the United States. She has written for such publications as *Somerset Studio*, *Altered Couture*, *Belle Armoire*, *Haute Handbags*, *Everyday Jewelry* and *Cenizo Journal* where she has a column on desert wisdom, plants and folktales. You can find her jewelry and supplies at mariefrench.etsy.com or inspiritu.etsy.com and you can read of her healing and sacred art at inspiritustudios.blogspot.com.

127

DISCOVER MORE INSPIRATION WITH THESE NORTH LIGHT TITLES.

A STRING OF EXPRESSION

June Roman

Discover how the self-expressive elements you put into works of art can be transferred into the jewelry you create. Author June Roman shares how she draws inspiration from her own journal pages and guides you through the process of using colors, textures, symbolism and more to express yourself in beautiful jewelry. *A String of Expression* takes you on a journey through five chapters—each exploring a unique facet of our world such as the colors we love, the places we've traveled, the people who have inspired us and the fantasies we keep tucked deep in our hearts.

ISBN-13: 978-1-60061-791-1
ISBN-10: 1-60061-791-3
paperback, 128 pages, Z5250

OBJECTS OF REFLECTION

Annie Lockhart

Objects of Reflection embodies visual journaling disguised in the form of dimensional assemblage by creating art that is so personal it resembles a page from the artist's journal. Inspiration pours from every page of the book through a gallery of projects designed by the author. In addition, over 20 step-by-step techniques include tips for attaching elements with simple materials like string, wire and tape, aging objects, adding texture with modeling paste and more. You'll learn how to tell your own stories through your art as you turn symbolic objects into your "words."

ISBN-13: 978-1-60061-331-9
ISBN-10: 1-60061-331-4
paperback, 128 pages, Z2974

SEMIPRECIOUS SALVAGE

Stephanie Lee

Create clever and creative jewelry that tells a story of where it's been, as metal, wire and beads are joined with found objects, some familiar and some unexpected. You'll learn the ins and outs of cold connections, soldering, aging, using plaster, resins and more, all in the spirit of a traveling expedition.

ISBN-13: 978-1-60061-019-6
ISBN-10: 1-60061-019-6
paperback, 128 pages, Z1281

DUSTY DIABLOS

Michael deMeng

Bring your artistic yearnings and sense of adventure along on a journey to the land of Dusty Diablos. Inspiration seeps from every page, and inside here you'll find: a tasty mix of ancient folklore (from the ancient metropolis of Teotihuacán to the miracle witnessed by Juan Diego); colorful pop culture (who knew that Western-Horror was its own film genre or that there's an entire island overrun with misfit dolls?) and informative art-making how-tos (like the Tricky Burnt Paper Routine and crafting your own Nicho). Join author Michael deMeng on an artist's pilgrimage south of the border and experience a culture as rich as it is beautiful and as genuine and down-to-earth as it is humorous and fascinating.

ISBN-13: 978-1-60061-350-0
ISBN-10: 1-60061-350-0
paperback, 146 pages, Z3606

128

These and other fine F+W Media titles are available from your local craft retailer, bookstore, online supplier, or, visit our website at www.mycraftivitystore.com.